...nar School, October, 1920.

WGS | A History of Wolverhampton's Grammar School

WGS | A History of Wolverhampton's Grammar School

Paul Cheeseright

WGS: A History of Wolverhampton's Grammar School
© Wolverhampton Grammar School

First published in 2010 by James & James (Publishers) Ltd,
a subsidiary of Third Millennium Information Limited.

JAMES
X
JAMES

2–5 Benjamin Street
London
United Kingdom
EC1M 5QL
www.tmiltd.com

ISBN 978 1 903942 98 7

British Library Cataloguing in Publication Data
A CIP catalogue record for this book is available from the
British Library.

Project edited by Susan Millership
Designed by Susan Pugsley
Production by Bonnie Murray
Reprographics by Studio Fasoli, Italy
Printed by Printer Trento, Italy

PICTURE ACKNOWLEDGEMENTS
Most of the images are from the School archives and modern
photograph collection. WGS and TMI would also like to thank
the following for permission to reproduce material: p 19 ©
Andrew Rowland; p 28 Bridgeman Art; p 44 (top) Ray Jones
(Marston Wolverhampton Heritage Trust); p 44 (left) and p 62
(right) Mary Evans Picture Library; p 82 Topfoto.

Although every reasonable effort has been made to identify
copyright holders of images used in this book, the publishers
will welcome any further information.

CONTENTS

	Foreword by Dr Simon Walford, chairman of governors	6
	Author Acknowledgements	9
	Introduction by Vincent Darby, head	12
Chapter One	The First Centuries (1512–1875)	18
Chapter Two	Climbing through the Ranks (1875–1923)	36
Chapter Three	Warren Derry: the Booth preamble, peace, war and control (1923–56)	54
Chapter Four	The Uneven Road to Independence (1956–78)	74
Chapter Five	Striking Out Alone: Stocks introduces the Hutton years (1978–90)	90
Chapter Six	Breaking with the Past: the Trafford years (1990–2008)	106
Chapter Seven	Towards the 500th Anniversary	124
Appendix I	The Headmasters	136
Appendix II	Helpful Books	138
	Index	142

FOREWORD
FROM THE CHAIRMAN OF THE GOVERNORS

Five hundred years of history is quite a daunting inheritance for those who lead and teach in school now. Yet it is an interesting story of mixed fortunes and occasional moments of great inspiration and determination, sustaining and improving the School to its present strength. That drive to create the best possible environment for the education of today's pupils is as strong as ever. So too is a commitment to remain forward thinking about how we will leave the School to future generations.

Five hundred years of history is mostly irrelevant when in the optimistic flush of youthful endeavour! Yet I hope that our current pupils will be touched with pride when they read about their educational heritage. I hope it will instil a real sense of responsibility to use wisely the opportunity for their own enhancement and the common good.

To all who read this book, I hope you find a connection with our roots in the small beginnings of accessible education and will celebrate with us the growing enlightenment and continuing success of our mission over those 500 years of history!

Dr Simon Walford
Chair of governors

Detail from marble fireplace in the Gerald Mander Room.

AUTHOR ACKNOWLEDGEMENTS

The first chapter relies heavily on the work of Gerald Mander: his history of the School, taken to the first years of the 20th century, is an act of antiquarian devotion, which would be difficult and pointless to duplicate. Other books which have been of great assistance in putting the School's development into context are Chris Upton's *A History of Wolverhampton* and Nicholas Timmins's *The Five Giants*, a biography of the welfare state. With other books, they are listed in the Appendix. Quotations in the text are acknowledged by the surname of the author.

Wolverhampton Grammar School has a valuable archive, pulled together first by Deirdre Linton, who compiled a very useful pictorial history, and latterly by Lynne Johnson. This book would have been impossible without this collection of School documents, not least *The Wulfrunian*, the school magazine started in the late 19th century. Wolverhampton City Council, on its website, has both an historical archive and a trove of contemporary information.

Especially for the later chapters, I am vastly indebted to a host of people at, and associated with, the School. They have been generous with their time and expertise: the School is a very hospitable place. I thank Nic Anderson, Jann Boss, Robert Brandon, Connie Brough, Florence and John Darby, Vincent Darby, Madeleine Drew, Mark Hand, Gail Hill, John Johnson, Lynne Johnson, David Lambourne, Deirdre Linton, Gareth Phillips, Anthony Stocks, Bernard Trafford, Ian Tyler, Simon Walford and Malcolm Ward.

At Third Millennium Publishing and James & James Publishers, Hamish MacGibbon, Christopher Fagg and Susan Millership nursed the project with their customary skill and sensitivity and Susan Pugsley has designed a beautiful book. They provided invaluable support and I am grateful for it.

Paul Cheeseright

The three crests adorning the main entrance to the School.

Overleaf: Aerial view of the School and surrounding area.

INTRODUCTION
BY VINCENT DARBY, HEAD

Like the town in which he was born, Sir Stephen Jenyns' fortune was built on the flourishing local wool trade. Thus, when he became Lord Mayor of London in 1509, Jenyns was determined to give something back to his hometown and so it was that in 1512, 'a faire Grammar-Schoole' for the instruction of boys in 'good morals and learning' opened in St John's Street in the heart of the town.

Today, as it approaches its 500th anniversary, Wolverhampton Grammar School is almost unrecognisable from the original foundation. For instance, the balcony in St Peter's Church was built in 1610 to accommodate all 60 boys in the school. Today WGS boasts 650 students, a third of them girls, and they fill the entire church. Similarly, in 1875, WGS moved from its cramped location in the town to the leafy splendour of Compton Road. And yet, despite expansion, relocation and the enormity of the changes that the School has experienced, our Founder's original aims of 'good morals and learning' are still at the heart of all we do.

Indeed, these values and strong sense of purpose have helped WGS to overcome many challenges in its history. Massive social, industrial and educational upheaval; the breakdown of relations with the School's founding fathers, the Merchant Taylors'; the impact of two World Wars and the political attack on grammar schools in the 1970s, have all been endured and survived. In fact, with each crisis, WGS became stronger and has blossomed into a very busy, happy and extremely successful independent school.

Much of the credit for the success of WGS is down to a cast of unsung heroes but, as with any history, some characters stand out. In particular, WGS has been fortunate to have attracted a series of charismatic and visionary headmasters, beginning with Thomas Beach in 1856. It was Beach who established the School's reputation for academic excellence which, under Warren Derry, saw WGS named as one of the top grammar schools in England. Ernest Taylor built on that reputation and his successor, Tony Stocks, led the fight against closure. Patrick Hutton saw the School safely through to full independence in 1979 and, under Bernard Trafford, WGS became fully co-educational, opened the OpAL programme and the innovative Big Six year group.

WGS has always welcomed students from a wide variety of backgrounds, from prominent local business families such as the Manders and the Marstons, to youngsters from very humble homes. Many of these Old Wulfrunians have gone

Mr Darby with pupils.

Opposite page: The weather vane on Big School.

on to achieve great things, amongst them John Abernethy the eminent surgeon; AET Benson, chief secretary of Nigeria; Norman Brook, secretary to the cabinet and chief of the BBC; WAS Hewins, first director of the London School of Economics; Mervyn King, governor of the Bank of England; John Lapsley, air marshal in the RAF; Stanley Mason, writer and poet; diplomat David Wright, and RW Moore, classical scholar, author and headmaster of Harrow school.

These men typify the outstanding education provided by WGS – an education that was anything but narrowly scholastic. Indeed, whilst the School has continually sought to improve its record in examination results and university entrance, it has also developed a fine reputation for sport, drama and music. The School's many strengths and friendly atmosphere were highlighted in the Inspection Report of 2007 and, as WGS approaches its 500th anniversary, it is justifiably proud of its tradition of excellence and can look forward to the future with real confidence.

Nowhere is this confidence more evident than in the School's exciting capital development programme and

commitment to increasing its student bursary fund in time for the Quincentenary in 2012.

At the heart of these plans is the intention to open a junior school – hardly a revolutionary idea since there was a junior school accommodated in the large Victorian house that stood in the school grounds until 1944. However, the welcome return of 7–10 year olds will be accompanied in this first phase of development by the creation of a new suite for languages in the old gym/art block and a superb sports pavilion at the rear of the Derry Hall. This will be followed by a second phase when the School will be focusing on new facilities for the Sciences and Humanities. WGS is also seeking to increase the number of bursaries available to bright and talented students whose parents would otherwise be unable to afford to send their children to the School.

A campaign to help fund these tremendous initiatives is due to be launched to coincide with the year of celebration for the Quincentenary beginning on Founder's Day, November 2011. Thus, the 500th anniversary will see WGS strengthening its role as a beacon of academic excellence while also looking

to make the superb education it offers available to as many local children as possible, thereby restating its commitment to continue as Wolverhampton's grammar school.

While WGS looks back with pride on its distinguished history and rightly celebrates its many strengths and traditions, naturally, we thank the governors, headmasters, teachers, staff, parents, OWs and, above all, students who have helped to create the School's tremendous ethos and atmosphere. WGS has overcome much and, like the city it serves, has developed a resilience, strength and unique identity along the way.

Five hundred years on from its foundation, WGS is an extremely successful school looking towards the future with confidence and a determination to go on improving, to go on being Wolverhampton's grammar school and to go on building on the foundations of 'good morals and learning' that remain the cornerstone of life at WGS.

This history is dedicated to our predecessors whose commitment and leadership created the distinctive character of our School. It is also a tribute to all the boys and girls who have made, and will continue to make, WGS so special.

Vincent Darby
May 2010

Clockwise from top left: Students at work, 2009; Oxbridge Honours board, Big School; detail from the School's stained glass window in St Peter's Church.

Overleaf: Cricket on Moreton's Piece.

1 | THE FIRST CENTURIES (1512–1875)

Rushock parish church gazes over neat fields and woodland, here a crop, there livestock, occasional stands of trees. Nearby is Rushock Court, once the manor house but now retaining only the cellar from a dwelling of 500 years ago. They are the high points among gentle hills. The Worcestershire village of Chaddesley Corbett is near, but the area conveys prosperous solitude, unaffected by the expansion of adjacent towns: Kidderminster, Bromsgrove and Droitwich. Today Rushock parish is home to around 200 people, not many more than in the 16th century.

These lands, over 900 acres in a survey of 1595, gave financial support to Wolverhampton Grammar School for more than 400 years. For that, generations of scholars thank Sir Stephen Jenyns, the Dick Whittington figure who went from the countryside to London in search of fortune. He found it and became a grand person, warden of Merchant Taylors', one of the great City livery companies, and then Lord Mayor at the time of the enthronement of Henry VIII. But he did not forget his origins.

Jenyns came from Wolverhampton, born in 1448. What he gave back was the School: 'he gave to the town its earliest (as it is, now its principal) secular blessing', as Mander thought, noting that the Church, the traditional source of education, had made scant provision. (Gerald Mander's history of the School until the early 20th century remains the standard work

on the subject.) Jenyns provided a building in St John's Street, on the edge of the town, bordering on fields. Having purchased Rushock, he set aside the rental revenue to pay for a master and an assistant, called an usher. It was 1512.

John Nechells, the son-in-law of Jenyns and another Merchant Taylor, subsequently augmented the estate. Thomas Offley, the third Merchant Taylor in the list of original benefactors, took over administration of the trust set up to administer the estate and provide for the School. Later, in the early 17th century, Randolph Woolley, the earliest known boarder at the School, made his fortune as a clothier, became warden of Merchant Taylors' and made a bequest to improve the master's salary. By then Merchant Taylors' had experienced some of the pitfalls which punctuated its 253 years of active trusteeship at the School.

Opposite page: Chaddesley Corbett in Worcestershire – for over 400 years WGS was supported by farming revenue from a 900-acre estate in this area.

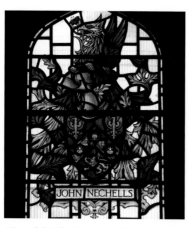

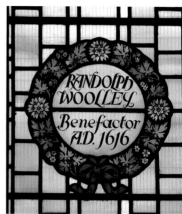

Three of the School's early benefactors are remembered in the stained glass in Big School: John Nechells, Sir Thomas Offley and Randolph Woolley, the School's first boarder, who, along with the School's founder, were all members of the Merchant Taylors' livery company.

The activities of Merchant Taylors' contributed to the educational ferment of the 16th century. Rich members founded schools in their places of birth; one established St John's College, Oxford. 'Have you noticed how many famous schools were founded in that century?' RW Moore, headmaster of Harrow School and once a pupil at Wolverhampton, asked Wolverhampton Grammar School parents, during a prize distribution in 1943. There were very few before, very few in the following two centuries; only in the 19th century did such a ferment resume.

Moore attributed this surge of activity to the Renaissance, an awakening from the Dark Ages. The idea was to advance civilization and to do this it was necessary to recover the lost culture and science of the Greeks. The route to the Greeks was through classical Latin, as opposed to the medieval variety. But there was an indigenous element too. This centred on the Reformation and the spread of Protestantism, which in turn tied in to the desire to have an English bible, which all could read.

After payment of a modest capitation fee, Wolverhampton boys would have access to a typical 16th-century curriculum, based on Latin, Greek and religious instruction; the aim of the founder was 'the instruction of boys in good morals and learning'. The Bishop of Lichfield licensed the schoolmasters, denoting an ecclesiastical influence which hovered over the administration of the School until the 19th century, when, for the first time, the trustees appointed a headmaster who was not a Church of England clergyman.

This influence was a potential source of conflict. The Church and the pattern of thinking – that set out by Moore – changed less quickly than Wolverhampton itself. When Jenyns started the School, the town was hardly less remote than Rushock. It was not important enough for the competing armies in the Civil War of the mid-17th century to do more than pass through – at, however, considerable cost to the townsfolk. By 1750 the estimated population had reached only 7,454. As Court, an historian of Midlands industry, observed, Wolverhampton was avoided by main roads; both it and nearby Walsall remained without adequate communication until well into the 18th century.

Yet, in this quiet patch of rural England, technically minded entrepreneurs had started the process which became the Industrial Revolution. Coal had been dug in Bilston and Wednesfield, Wolverhampton's neighbours, even when Jenyns

IN 1512 SIR STEPHEN JENYNS
— LORD MAYOR OF LONDON —
FOUNDED WOLVERHAMPTON GRAMMAR SCHOOL IN
BUILDINGS ON THIS SITE. BETWEEN 1712 AND 1717
THEY WERE RECONSTRUCTED BY THE MERCHANT
TAYLORS COMPANY THE THEN TRUSTEES OF THE
SCHOOL AND SERVED THEIR ORIGINAL PURPOSE
UNTIL THE YEAR 1874 WHEN THE SCHOOL REMOVED
TO COMPTON ROAD. AFTER BEING PUT TO VARIOUS
USES THEY WERE DEMOLISHED IN 1964 AS PART
OF THE CENTRAL TOWN DEVELOPMENT SCHEME
BY MANDERS PROPERTY (WOLVERHAMPTON) LIMITED.

THIS TABLET WAS ERECTED BY THE GOVERNORS
OF WOLVERHAMPTON GRAMMAR SCHOOL.
HENRY HALLMARK - CHAIRMAN OF THE GOVERNORS.
ERNEST R. TAYLOR. M.A. — HEADMASTER.

Plaque commemorating the original site of the School in St John Street.

was a child. Soon blast furnaces and forges appeared, then Dudley claimed to have produced iron using coal and, in 1709, Darby produced iron using coke. Production expanded in the South Staffordshire coalfield. Wolverhampton and the towns of the English Midlands stood poised for the change from rural market to manufacturing centres. It was a moot point how an education based on Horace, Homer and holiness, and run by a clergyman, would survive in an age of new materialism.

Classics and business would clash later, but, for the years of the Merchant Taylors' trusteeship, problems were more likely to have a religious or clerical angle. For the most part, School and masters went their own way and when School and townsfolk were at ease with each other the trusteeship was easy to execute. That suited the trustees: contact was difficult and time-consuming with a visit from London during the early decades involving days of travel.

But problems flared and then the role of Merchant Taylors' would require more animation. It would find itself both arbitrator and negotiator in local strife between School and townsfolk and it would be called in for fresh finance. It would find itself in the courts defending its record of trusteeship. Mander's assessment was that, 'without doubt the people of Wolverhampton were imbued with a factious spirit when dealing with the trustees of their School'.

Some problems could be easily dealt with. Complaints about headmasters, either unpopular like Mr Raby in 1590, or manifestly inefficient like John Plymley a century later, could be resolved by dismissal. Equally with ushers like William Burton, dismissed in 1618, or William Smith, dismissed in 1627. But steering a course through competing religious interests was more difficult.

Drawing of the old school, 1714.

21

An 18th-century view of Dudley Castle Hill with signs of early industrial activity, illustrated by the plume of smoke rising from the kiln.

In the early 17th century, Richard Barnes, the headmaster, found himself the centre of an ugly Roman Catholic–Protestant squabble, a reflection of broader controversy. The basic question was whether Roman Catholic children, from what were called recusant families, should attend the School. Merchant Taylors', on advice from the Archbishop of Canterbury, incensed the recusants, among whom some, like the Levesons, were highly influential in Wolverhampton. They refused to allow the admission of recusant children unless their parents frequented the Church of England. Faced by what Barnes called 'hurly burly' with townsmen, a Merchant Taylors' deputation arrived to find Barnes more unpopular than it had realised and the School in bad shape. The situation was resolved by removing Barnes to an agreeably snug benefice in Kent, where he remained, evidently content, for the next 24 years. 'The opposition of the townsmen yielded to the tact of the Merchants', Mander commented.

Interestingly, these religious divisions did not burst out during the convulsions of the Civil War between a Roman Catholic monarch and Protestant parliamentarians. Wolverhampton, conveniently out of the way and unfortified, remained neutral. Hence the School escaped unscathed, although Francis Storre, the usher, found it convenient to absent himself during a brief royalist occupation after making some indiscreet remarks favouring parliamentarians. Daniel

Rawlett continued peaceably as headmaster until 1658 having succeeded where others failed, according to Mander, 'to steer a middle course for 27 years and six months through civil strife and religious animosity'. In fact, the School was at a low ebb and not many years would pass before Merchant Taylors' would have to resume the legal defence of its position.

What appears to have been an underlying sense of grievance in Wolverhampton found expression in a bill of complaint entered by six citizens against Merchant Taylors' at the Court of Chancery in 1626. They charged that Merchant Taylors' appropriated Rushock funds for their own use, the rents on the estate were too high and the schoolmasters appointed were unfit for their job. The Court agreed in part, specifying that rents should go to the use of the school. After the Civil War, dissatisfaction bubbled to the surface again. 'The inhabitants of the town had continued their want of faith in the Merchant Taylors', Mander wrote. 'It was the usual cry for freedom and progress, supported by those who wanted something for nothing, and discountenanced by the conservatives, in this case the royalists and Roman Catholics.' Thus, the same problems and the same arguments had another airing in Chancery during 1684–5, without any great effect.

These were the rivalries and resentments of a small (but growing) community transformed into a loss of temper. The School had a niche in the community but the numbers

The gallery at
St Peter's Church.

involved during the early centuries were never great. The
earliest surviving list of pupils, from September 1609,
registered 69 boys of whom 28 were aged 11–18 with the
headmaster and 41 were 6–13 with the usher. When Merchant
Taylors' during 1610, in an act of generosity recognised by the
townfolk, paid for a gallery in St Peter's Collegiate Church for
the use of the whole School, it could accommodate 60, a sure
sign that the trustees did not expect the School to expand.
Indeed, the buildings in St John's Street would have been hard
pressed to cope.

Numbers fluctuated: up when the headmaster was
energetic, conscientious and locally respected, down when
the headmaster was the opposite. With Rawlett as a rather
passive headmaster during the Civil War period, numbers
slipped to under 40. In the years before Merchant Taylors'
surrendered the trusteeship, there were fewer than 25 dayboys
and five boarders. Early instruction of these pupils was largely
oral, although textbooks seem to have become more common
by the end of the 17th century. From 1616, pupils faced
examinations, but it seems doubtful that the School ever
became an intellectual powerhouse before the 19th century.
One of the complaints against Plymley, before he lost his

A gargoyle in St Peter's Church of Richard Barnes, one of the School's
early headmasters.

23

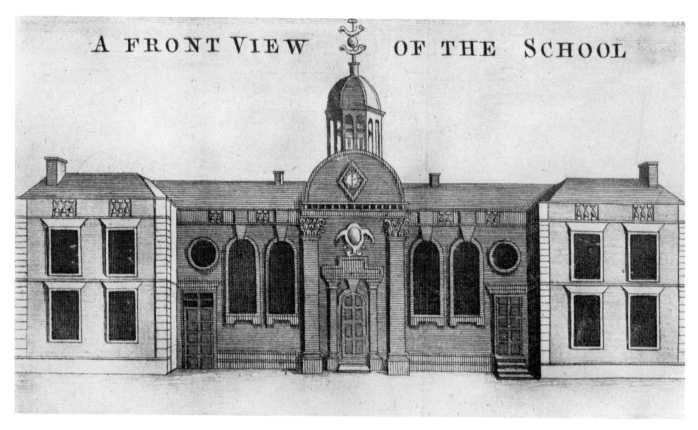

A FRONT VIEW OF THE SCHOOL

The front of the School, 1750.

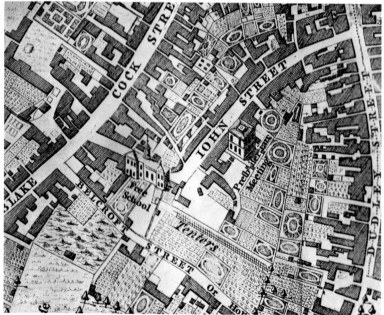

A map by Isaac Taylor showing the School's location in 1750.

But Wolverhampton did not stand out from the national trend. Griffith, in a 19th-century assessment, drew attention to 'the bad management of grammar schools', citing Lord Kenyon, sitting in the Court of Queen's Bench, that 'the grammar schools were reduced to a lamentable state, that they were merely empty walls without scholars, and that everything was neglected but the receipt of emoluments'. Mander's analysis of the problems of maladministration at Wolverhampton concerned what he classified as a town decayed in structure, energy and morality, few visitations from Merchant Taylors', a School from which low standards were expected and received, and the pursuit of outside interests by the headmaster and usher – they frequently had other ecclesiastical duties and benefits. He also noted the running complaints about the state of the School's building.

Dissatisfaction in Wolverhampton burst into a direct appeal in Chancery for the removal of Merchant Taylors' as trustees, during 1757 and again in 1778, when all the old grievances emerged for a rehearsal of the established arguments. But by this time Merchant Taylors' had had enough and prepared to retreat. Mander stated that Merchant Taylors'

post, was that he was lax in attendance: on enquiry Merchant Taylors' found scholars who complained of more play than learning. Only four went to either of the country's two universities, Oxford and Cambridge, in four years.

24

Document from 1784 transferring the school from the control of Merchant Taylors' to new trustees.

accepted the inevitable, 'since they had for 140 years past at different times been harassed by different sets of inhabitants of the town of Wolverhampton, and were generally out of pocket, they were "willing and desirous", after receiving satisfaction for their expenditure, "to be discharged from the care and management of the said school and premises"'. In 1784 Merchant Taylors' handed over to new trustees.

The ending for Merchants Taylors' may have been lengthy and messy: what they had founded proved difficult to keep. They may have lost patience eventually, but the fact was that they had kept a school running since 1512. By passing on the baton of care they could, if they chose, retain an association of friendship without the problems of responsibility. Such is the case 300 years further on. But then, in the closing years of the 18th century, the School stood on the cusp of change – change

which would propel it falteringly over the next decades into the educational elite.

The new trustees came largely from the country gentry, an odd selection given the changes to the character of Wolverhampton. By the late 18th century, noted Chris Upton, a local historian and chronicler of Wolverhampton affairs, the agricultural origins of the town had become a distant memory. Metalworkers had been drawn to the town towards the end of the late 16th century as easy access to coal made Wolverhampton one of England's earliest industrial centres. The town emerged as a specialist in the manufacture of locks and buckles – there were 118 lockmakers in 1770, mentioned Upton – but it also saw the rapid development of japanning, the name given to a technique of lacquering, a trade where, Court suggested, the processes are simple and the design

William Robertson, Headmaster 1768–83.

Far right: John Abernethy was a pupil at the School during Robertson's time. He went on to become a distinguished anatomist and founder of St Bartholomew's Medical School.

WILLIAM ROBERTSON *D.D. of Wolverhampton 1767. Aged 62.*

difficult. Much of this activity went on in small shops but trade tended to be dominated by large houses like those of the Molineux and Ryton families, both of which, incidentally, had representatives in the group which pursued Merchant Taylors' in Chancery.

In neither general nor particular terms did the new trustees take over at an easy time. They had scarcely been ensconced when war with France and the shrinking of overseas markets, on which Wolverhampton was heavily dependent for 75 per cent of its manufactured goods, caused what Upton called an 'unprecedented time of economic depression in Britain'. In the town, the numbers of indoor poor doubled between 1794 and 1797.

The trustees found the School in a poor state at a time when it had to contend with competition: a new Roman Catholic school had started at Sedgley Park in 1763 and had proved instantly successful. Shortly after that, the respected William Robertson became headmaster at Wolverhampton and for a time numbers increased. But as he aged and found his gout increasingly wearisome, the numbers dropped again, and he died just before the new trustees assumed responsibility. The School's buildings were in such a poor state that the new trustees had to start repairs and refurbishment immediately; they wanted, in any case, to expand the premises, over the

opposition, it appeared, of Lord Thurlow. 'There was not a vast concourse at the School in the interval between Dr Robertson's death and the re-opening of the School in 1785', said Mander gently. In truth, the School had touched its nadir. 'The boys had in fact dwindled to two, Thomas Savage and William Chrees.'

But the trustees, many of whom quickly found it inconvenient to attend twice-yearly meetings at the Swan Inn, tilted optimistically at the future. They decided in a formulation of new rules for the School that the schooling itself would be free and 'that the headmaster and the usher shall not be obliged to teach more than one hundred and fifty boys'; the headmaster could take in up to 40 boarders and the usher 12, a handy source of extra income for both of them. In fact, the total number of pupils was just under 100 before parents started withdrawing their boys, evidently feeling that the nature of the education was not fitting for their economic status – what Mander called 'the commercial instincts of the parents'. By the first years of the 19th century the number of day boys had fallen to 22.

Mander is generally dismissive of the new trustees. 'The state of the School after it had been 20 years under its new governors is but evidence of the Merchant Taylors' integrity in the past.' The fact was they took over the School when it was in a poor state and seemed unable, any more than Merchant Taylors', initially to ameliorate the situation. Yet their early actions had a profound importance for later development. They quickly decided, with what Mander called 'generous support', to create an extra schoolroom for a 'commercial' department, to appoint a second usher to teach writing, arithmetic and mathematics and to employ part-time masters for drawing and for French and German. This had two results.

First, it cracked the traditional mould of education based on classics and catechism; it started the process of pushing aside Church influence over a secular institution. Second, it recognised that, if the School wanted a prosperous future, it had to provide education which appeared relevant to the needs of the local community. There is, for example, an obvious link between the teaching of drawing and the trade of japanning. Both results together brought Wolverhampton into line with wider educational trends.

In his history of the welfare state Nicholas Timmins observed that, going into the 19th century, only seven per cent of children attended day school and schooling remained voluntary, but, he noted, the Industrial Revolution produced a demand for better-educated workers. The government was slow to recognise the growing demand and did not move to use public money for education until 1833. By this time not only had schools like Wolverhampton Grammar School acted on their own initiative, but also workers had opted for self-help by forming mechanics' institutes. In any case, the Grammar School had long since lost its exclusive position in the town. By the middle of the century, according to Mason's list, Wolverhampton had 13 other schools of varying types and size.

The town, to be sure, was caught in massive change. The population started to rise quickly in the second half of the 18th century, more than doubling between 1750 and 1821 to over 18,000, but then the pace accelerated and in the next 80 years it more than quintupled to exceed 94,000 by 1901. More people, more factories, haphazard construction. Upton quoted an official report of the 1840s which drew attention to poor building and no mains drainage. For employees of large and small manufactures alike, social and working conditions were at best bleak. Tempers could fray: public disorder remained one of the chief concerns of the authorities, Philips commented, noting how troops opened fire on metalworkers in 1835.

This was not an environment any school would choose. For the new trustees, the physical position and condition of the School remained a besetting problem for three-quarters of the 19th century. Parents held back from sending their boys to a

Schoolboys in the playground, 1795.

location which, although once semi-rural, had been caught up in urban expansion: it was insalubrious on the outside and decrepit on the inside. Thomas Campbell, the headmaster during the middle years of the century, found the place impossible:

> Its space is cramped, confined and ill-arranged; its air is heavily charged with the reek of japan manufactories and chemical works; its view is bounded on all sides by objects of insupportable ugliness and dullness [sic]; and its neighbourhood is infested with every sort of nuisance – moral and physical; the accommodation in the way of schoolrooms etc. is very insufficient; the second master's house is unhealthy from irremediable damp; the headmaster's house, though comfortable and roomy enough for private purposes, is quite unfit in its arrangements for the reception of boarders.

Unsurprisingly, the School limped along, and, it appeared, to no great effect. Mason classified it as 'moribund'; William

Jones, later a mayor of the town, declared that, at the time of incorporation as a borough (1848), 'the School became almost useless to the inhabitants of Wolverhampton'.

Two headmasters dominated the School's affairs during the first half of the 19th century: William Tindall to 1830 and William White from then to 1855. Tindall, who had joined the School as usher in 1785 and later became the headmaster, complained to the Charity Commissioners in 1820 that the majority of boys coming to the School left at 13 or 14, as parents considered them adequately qualified for the trade occupations to which they were destined. Indeed, the average number of students during Tindall's period, to 1830, moved between 50 and 60. What parents wanted, according to the results of an 1820 public meeting, was an auxiliary school to fit children for the upper school and, furthermore, less reliance on classical education which was deemed of limited benefit.

There seems little evidence that anything much changed. Rather, after Tindall, the trustees appointed the unbending William White, described by Mander as 'a conservative man for an antiquated system'. An anonymous former pupil

Homework journal, 1832.

recalled that his 'favourite method of expressing disapproval was to fling pewter inkstands at the boys, first carefully removing the inkpots'; his assistant, John Gooch, 'swore by the cane, and his boys swore at it'. White directed that there would be no admissions outside the 8–12 age range and 'in no case in which the parent is not of ability to purchase the necessary books'. Those anxious for a free education simply went to one of the national schools which came into Wolverhampton from 1832.

Trustees became more animated in their attention to the School, when, in 1840, 196 citizens sent them a memorandum protesting about the severity of discipline in the School, an indication of which was White's offer of a reward for the disclosure of those who had gradually stolen eight of his canes. 'An exceptional attendance of trustees took place', Mander reported. More important for the longer run, the 196 wanted the School to run concurrent systems of education, one for classical literature, the other for general commercial purposes, that is English, grammar, history, geography, writing, accounts and mathematics. The Diocesan Board of Education had its say, calling predictably for more religious instruction, but the trustees evidently paid less attention to the Board than the 196, a further instance of the waning Church influence. The School, in fact, broadly adopted the suggestion of the new commercial course, without additional religious instruction. This had the simultaneous effect of mitigating slightly the traditional classical bias. The local response was quick: School numbers began to increase, reaching 123 by 1844. But the popularity proved short lived as the new system failed to live up to parental expectation, causing numbers to halve.

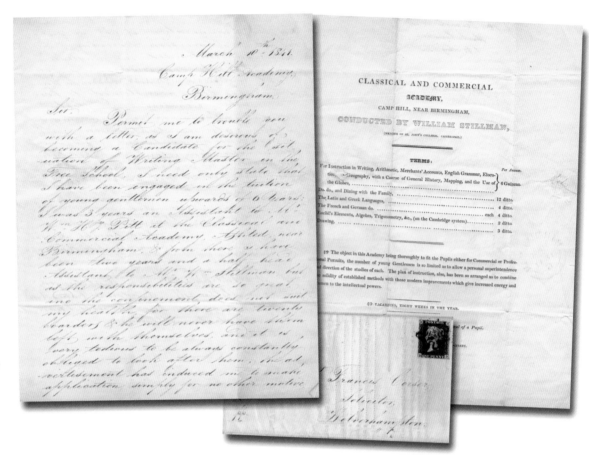

A letter applying for the position of Writing Master, 1841. The letter was written on the back of a sheet publicising a commercial academy that prepared pupils for 'Commercial or Professional Pursuits'.

Although the School nodded in the direction of vocational skills, the prevailing thinking about the nature of education did not favour commercial outcomes. By mid-century, schools in the private sector looked to Thomas Arnold and the example of Rugby, which, said Timmins, was hierarchical, games-playing, privileged, classics-based and robustly Christian. Rugby wanted to produce public leaders, not private businessmen, still less tradesmen. Or, to put that another way, the thrust was precisely what the interested townsfolk of Wolverhampton had been seeking to tone down: it was not very helpful in the factory. But they did not give up, in a petition pressing the trustees not only to appoint more staff for French and drawing but also to make the School more efficient, 'more in accordance with the wants and spirit of the age'. The trustees refused to engage and referred the petition to the Court of Chancery.

In February 1854, the Court produced a scheme. The headmaster and usher should be both members of the established Church and graduates of Oxford, Cambridge or Durham, so little change there. Masters should be appointed for French, German, drawing and writing, as the petition had sought. Priority of admission should be granted to the boys of

Wolverhampton, which meant favouring local dayboys rather than country boarders; the boys should be eight years old; their numbers should not exceed 100, exclusive of boarders; and they should be able to read English. Costs to the parents would be an entry fee of £2 for each boy and a capitation fee of another £2 each half year.

The introduction of the new scheme, followed a year later by the appointment of Thomas Campbell as headmaster, hastened change, a move away from the doldrums of the previous 100 years. Mander had no doubt of that:

> *The ensuing ten years mark a period of transition; the growth of a modern grammar school, the winning of honour and respect. In ceasing to be 'free' the School was delivered from the lichen of timeworn associations, and a fresh start was possible for the gain of distinction.*

None of this came easily. Campbell's impact was swift: a library started, boys had to wear caps, but Church attendance ceased to be compulsory and new desks and benches appeared in the schoolrooms. A year after his arrival the School's roll had

extended to 81 dayboys and five boarders – but it proved too much and too quick and numbers dropped after it had been found that too many incompetent pupils had been admitted. But Campbell found the 1854 scheme of arrangement a straitjacket. There was no provision for new masters, fees could not be changed and neither could the curriculum. The system was so rigid and Campbell so dedicated that he provided for an assistant master out of his own pocket.

Campbell knew that the future of the School could not be assured unless it moved from St John Street. By 1858 he had won the agreement of the trustees, who proposed to finance a shift to 'a more healthy and commodious site' by selling the existing site, raising a mortgage and increasing the capitation fees. The trustees published a notice of intention in the *Wolverhampton Chronicle* and excited local controversy. The Town Council became interested but had no particular ideas. Blame for the state of School spread out: it was the buildings, argued some people; it was the curriculum, contended others. The trustees started to look for sites and almost purchased some land in 1861, but they could not agree among themselves, so the Charity Commissioners, who had to give their agreement, refused to become involved.

Meanwhile, examiners visiting the School consistently complained about its state. The early promise Campbell had seemed to offer started to disappear. Standards slipped: to

The front of the school in St John Street, 1854.

The Revd Thomas Campbell, Headmaster 1855–63.

service the education of boys in the upper school, he had to allow education in the lower to suffer with the result that in the commercial department half of the boys had no idea of figures, rather defeating the object of it. By 1861 Campbell seemed to have had enough. The trustees were no further advanced in the

A cartoon of Thomas Beach, Headmaster, 1865–89. Beach was a larger-than-life character who believed passionately in old-style, classical teaching. He resigned in disgust when the governors appointed the School's first science master.

down another scheme of arrangement, this time of more flexibility than that of 1854. There would be two departments, each under the headmaster's control, one dubbed English or commercial, the other classical and more advanced. Mander noted that one department would be preparatory for the other, meaning in effect an upper and a lower school, with the latter providing something of a general education before a later stress on the classics. The headmaster and the trustees could appoint assistants as they thought fit. Capitation fees went up but the trustees could provide free admission to promising boys. In addition, and this proved of immediate importance, the headmaster need not be a clergyman, another slight reduction of ecclesiastical influence, although he had to be a member of the Church of England.

Thomas Beach was the first layman to be headmaster. Chosen from 71 applicants, he arrived in 1865 with Henry Williams, a clergyman, as his second master. This marked the start of a new era. Beach propelled the School into the high ranks of the English educational system, giving it a name for scholastic prowess which it has constantly burnished. What he found in Wolverhampton was not immediately encouraging. Writing later in the School's magazine, a former pupil calling himself Tertiolulus recalled the old School

consisting of two rooms, the Big Room with its bare whitewashed walls and ceilings, its cracked and ill-repaired windows high up above the eyeline, here and there some old wainscot, the floor uneven and almost unsafe, and the still more dilapidated Writing Room, the whole situated in the dingy St John's Lane [sic], then … full of small houses and dingy evil-smelling courts, whose inhabitants were by no means of the best repute.

Beach had a good early career: a mathematics honours graduate from Cambridge, head of mathematics at Royal Grammar School, Lancaster, and a stand-in headmaster there. It seemed odd at first sight that he should want to live in Wolverhampton, described by the *Morning Chronicle* and quoted by Upton as 'a perfect desert of coal dust, mud and refuse', to take charge of an insalubrious School of troubled reputation. Years later, in a speech to former pupils, he acknowledged that there was nothing 'to cheer the heart of the newcomer' and that 'the local situation of the School

move to a new site, numbers of pupils had slipped and he had the offer of another post in Dunedin, New Zealand. So he left in 1863 but to a sad fate: his boat arrived in New Zealand only to have an accident at the port that killed him. William Wood became the temporary headmaster with a roll down to 42 boys.

Campbell's legacy was 'at least the nucleus and the organisation of a good school', as one visiting examiner put it. The nucleus strengthened in 1864 when the Court handed was sad beyond description'. But he offered three reasons for taking up the headmastership. The School was in the midst of dense population and from this came 'a vista of brilliant possibilities'; the School had a fair endowment, enough to tide over the first years of difficulty until the School's merits became known; he had been encouraged, he said, by the nature of the governing body.

Beach holds the pivotal position in the history of Wolverhampton Grammar School. Before him the School existed, under him it found life, after him it prospered. Unlike his predecessors who held other positions in the Church, Beach had only one focus of attention. The School became his life and his life became the School's. 'He believed in himself, he believed in the School, he believed in his boys', a former pupil remembered. By all accounts he was an exceptional schoolmaster, not a great scholar but, as one of those he taught had it, 'his forte as a teacher lay in the fact that he knew, as no man I have met since knew, how to impart, and drive into us, the knowledge that he possessed'. He drew great pleasure from the academic success of his boys. From them he expected absolute obedience. As one misbehaving culprit recalled, 'it was, as I have reason to believe, his firm opinion that there have been no good scholars since birch rods went out of schools and sentiment went in'. In any case, his manner demanded respect; he had 'an imposing presence, curious carmine-dyed hair'. He certainly was vain about his appearance. Contemporary accounts noted how he changed his whiskers and moustache in accordance with fashion. He favoured check trousers with his tailcoat but had a slightly unbalanced appearance with a large head and small legs.

Manifestly he also had great tact to accompany his sure purpose. He managed almost immediately to win the confidence of the trustees in a way which Campbell had never done. His position on the School's buildings was exactly the same – the location was impossible – but he managed to generate action where Campbell previously had failed. His position vis-à-vis the trustees strengthened with each year of academic success. From the start of his regime, pupil numbers had increased: 28 when he arrived, 77 in mid-summer 1865, 186 by 1867 and 201 by 1868. The School had reached, for it, the extraordinary position of having to turn away applicants. Along with that Beach could claim in a letter to the trustees 'the leading position which it has taken in the

public competitive examinations'. The sting in the tail, though, was Beach's warning that the teachers had been making exceptional efforts in the expectation that the state of affairs in St John Street would be temporary: 'I cannot conceal from you that I entertain grave fears as to whether I can count upon a continuance of the same strained effort on the part of my staff'. There it was laid out for the trustees: no move, no staff; no staff, no future.

Delays now came, not from the trustees, but from London where the Charity Commissioners held back approval for the move and construction of buildings suitable for 300 pupils until after the passage through Parliament of the Endowed Schools Bill. With Rupert Kettle in the chair, the trustees had sought first to buy a house and land of nine acres on Penn Road. Later, given approval by the Charity Commissioners in 1872, the trustees bought the present site of the School in April 1873; it was part of the old Merridale Farm and it cost £3027 16s. 8d., paid to Henry Owen, a merchant. The foundation stone for the new School went down in 1874. It had taken Beach nine years to go this far and it was about 40 years since a move had become necessary.

The Wulfrunian was first published in 1875 with the aim of fostering 'a unity of feeling and sense of fellowship, and the spread of that public spirit which ought to exist among us, by providing ourselves with a possession in which every boy may have a share and an interest'.

A fragment of carved masonry from the building in St John Street is now displayed outside the library at Compton Road.

Overleaf: The School celebrates Founder's Day in St Peter's Church.

2 | CLIMBING THROUGH THE RANKS (1875–1923)

The bells rang at the Collegiate Church, the Royal Standard was hoisted on the dome of the Wolverhampton Town Hall and on the new tower of Wolverhampton Grammar School. The procession started at the Town Hall and moved to the new premises of the School for the formal inauguration. Lord Wrottesley, the Lord Lieutenant, took the chair. The Mayor was in attendance and gave a sumptuous lunch at the Town Hall afterwards. A deputation from Merchant Taylors', the City of London guild and original benefactor of the School, was there to see the flowering of their original intent. The date was 15 October 1875. Thomas Beach, the headmaster for a decade, had climbed to the pinnacle of his career.

For Beach, the day marked the point where he could start to use the surroundings of the School and not fight them. He could enlarge the work of the School from the academic

Opposite page: Lessons took place in the Great Hall, later called Big School.

Thomas Beach, Headmaster 1865–89.

to the social and cultural, he could start to fashion a school with the attributes recognisable in a leading 20th-century institution. But the day had a wider significance. It denoted the acceptance by the town of Wolverhampton that the School had the unchallenged purpose of educating the clever cream of its youth, of providing for new generations of leaders. The days of sniping at the School for the insalubrious nature of its premises and the inadequacy of its teaching had passed, even if the type of education it provided remained a source of debate. In short, Rupert Kettle, the chairman of the governors and a prosperous local lawyer, and Beach himself, had succeeded in embedding the School in the community.

This success had immediate importance. When Kettle set out the financial details of the School's move at the inauguration ceremony, he estimated the final cost of land, buildings, furniture and fittings at £20,000. Half of that came from funds the School governors had in hand and from a 30-year mortgage on the Rushock estate, the original bequest of Stephen Jenyns and Merchant Taylors'. The rest would come from the sale of the St John Street building and from public subscription which by the time of the inauguration had reached £3,700. This would be the first of a succession of appeals to the public for funds over the next 100 years and they always found a generous response. This would not have been the case had the tentacles of the School not spread through the community: with former pupils in positions of responsibility across Wolverhampton's commercial sector, the School had a strong base for fundraising.

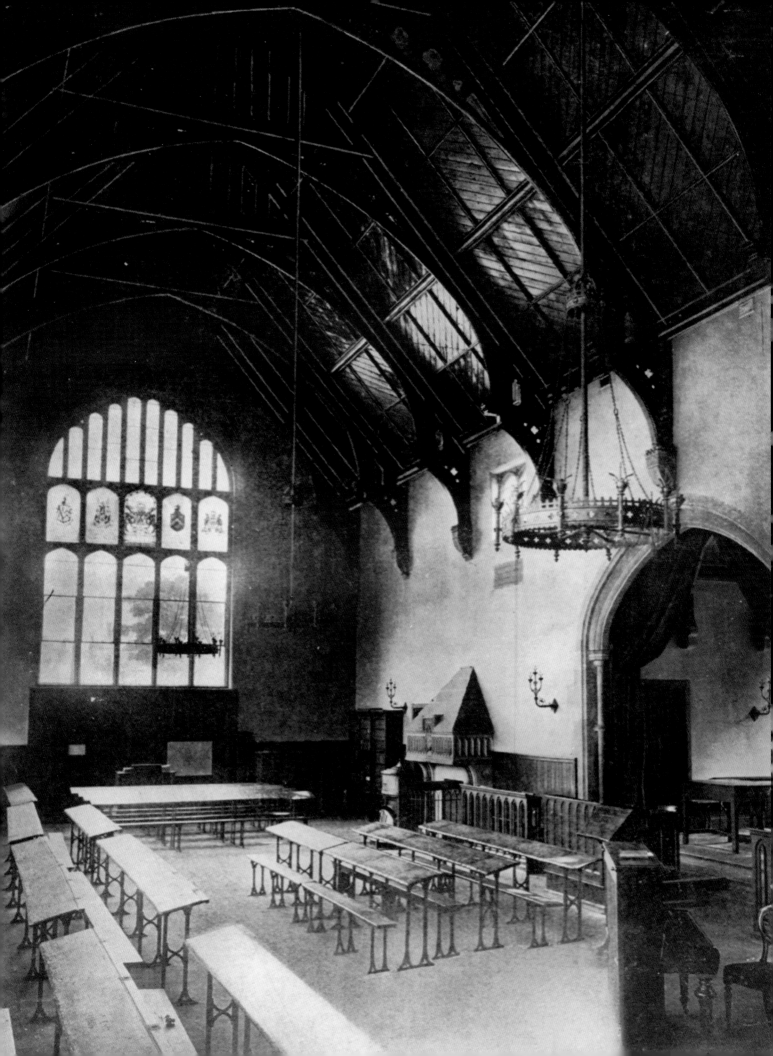

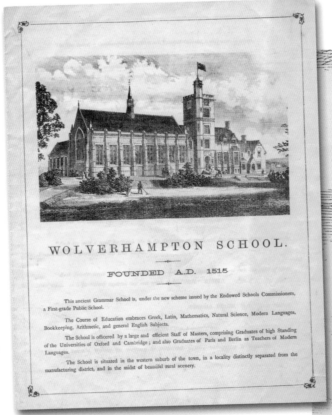

WOLVERHAMPTON SCHOOL.

FOUNDED A.D. 1515

This ancient Grammar School is, under the new scheme issued by the Endowed Schools Commissioners, a First-grade Public School.

The Course of Education embraces Greek, Latin, Mathematics, Natural Science, Modern Languages, Bookkeeping, Arithmetic, and general English Subjects.

The School is officered by a large and efficient Staff of Masters, comprising Graduates of high standing of the Universities of Oxford and Cambridge; and also Graduates of Paris and Berlin as Teachers of Modern Languages.

The School is situated in the western suburb of the town, in a locality distinctly separated from the manufacturing district, and in the midst of beautiful rural scenery.

The School's first prospectus at Compton Road highlighted the spaciousness of the new buildings and its rural setting. Far right: Architect's drawing of the new school.

The new School's first prospectus went to some pains to dissociate the School from the less desirable elements of Wolverhampton's industrial existence. On Compton Road, 'the School is situated in the western suburb of the town, in a locality distinctly separated from the manufacturing district, and in the midst of beautiful rural scenery'. Now, instead of being part of the cramped pattern of the urban street, the School had space to breathe on a site of 6.5 acres. One building, stretched to be sure, provided all the accommodation, a Great Hall which was the schoolroom, later to be called Big School, rooms for boarders with their stately entrance under the tower and a house for the headmaster.

Beach began to put in place some of the accoutrements of a major school. The first edition of *The Wulfrunian*, the school magazine, came out in autumn 1875 wanting, it said, 'to do something towards the fostering of a unity of feeling and sense of fellowship'; it would be 'a chronicle in which to record the triumphs and honours'. This misfired as lack of support caused it to fold in 1876, but a second attempt in 1882 proved successful and the magazine exists to this day. Its tone and contents have varied erratically over the years; sometimes it has

A cricket team in 1890 – at this time boys and masters played together in important matches.

tried to initiate. Association football and athletics followed. The Debating Society 'opened with eclat', *The Wulfrunian* reported in 1885, and started with 70 members. During the early years attendance usually held at over 90 and the meetings were 'conspicuous by the absence of any disorder or rowdyism', which was not always the case later on. The subjects – formation of a tennis club, the Irish Question, the Channel Tunnel, town improvement, for example – reflected internal concerns and external interests.

The stress on academic results did not diminish, however. Beach continued in the new School what he had started in the old. In 1885, he reported to parents, in the university local examinations, 74 per cent of junior candidates passed in the nation as a whole, but at Wolverhampton Grammar School the percentage was 85.7. In the senior examination, nationally, 62.7 per cent passed, but, at the School, all the candidates passed. 'This bore evidence that they were again the premier school as regarded their senior scholars.'

These scholars had a privileged existence compared with what was happening around them. Wolverhampton and the adjacent areas had by the latter part of the 19th century become a national workshop but at a price of social deprivation and physical depredation. Some scholars were acutely aware of this and vented distaste in *The Wulfrunian*. One, unnamed, wrote:

> *For the song of birds, we now hear the screech of the steam engine; the murmuring stream has become a foul slimy ditch, and thick clouds of smoke hang for ever over the land.*

RM Smyth, angry at the grotesque Black Country, saw

> *a tract covered with mountains of dross, heaved and contorted as though Earth herself frowned, whilst hideous erections, foul and blackened, pour forth flames and smoke, covering the sky with a dark haze by day, while by night the lurid fires cast upon it a flickering glow like the reflection of some gigantic conflagration.*

Oxbridge Old Wulfrunian dinner, 1900.

been content to be a recital of activities and achievements, at other times it has been a source of creative writing, in some years a means of communicating with parents and friends. Its appearance changed too, from the fusty and closely printed to the exuberantly coloured. As the years passed it had more to report.

Beach, in the style of Thomas Arnold of Rugby, laid stress on sports and cultural activities. The School began to build a reputation for sporting prowess, starting with cricket where Beach built on what Thomas Campbell, his predecessor, had

In fact, the School moved to Compton Road roughly at the same time as the start of what became known as the Great Depression when markets fell away, production dropped and product prices declined. Barnsby asserted that the Great Depression devastated the iron industry, as it did coal mining, what had been the mainstays of the Wolverhampton industrial economy. The ironmasters started closing their works from 1879, so that only 24 out of 147 furnaces were in blast. It is true that new industry arrived in the second half of the century: Upton reported how the Great Western Railway factory, making locomotives, quickly became the biggest employer in the town. But general recovery had to wait until the 1890s.

The Great Depression quickened official interest in education. There were, as Timmins made clear, concerns about the general ignorance of the British workman. At the same time, the direct involvement of the state in education – through the Elementary Education Act of 1870 and local government changes which from 1889 allowed authorities to provide technical education – produced pressure for a stronger scientific element in the traditional curriculum. This impinged directly on the School when, as Mander wrote, 'the Charity Commissioners advocated a change in the curriculum to the further advancement of the modern side'; this would involve the appointment of a science master. Some of the governors, local businessmen for the most part, felt the same way. This, then, was a reiteration of the arguments about what the School should teach, that had punctuated the 18th and early

19th centuries, setting townsfolk against the School. Further, it exposed a flaw in Beach and led to his downfall.

Beach was never a man to tolerate interference in what he saw as his domain. He was at once intellectually arrogant and technically conservative. One of those he taught was Herbert Flewker who would later recall 'a man of the old school, he hated innovations and liked to live up to the reputation: anything new was an encroachment on the old order, therefore he hated bicycles'. For him the appointment of a new science master was a step too far. He resigned, rapidly to become a favourite in Wolverhampton luncheon and dinner circles.

However sad the method of his departure, Beach left a great legacy. He may now be relegated to a distant past, known only by photograph and caricature, both severe in demeanour but with funny whiskers, yet, more than any other figure, he is responsible for defining the future shape of Wolverhampton Grammar School. The headmasters who followed shaped traditions on his foundations.

The shaping did not start immediately. In selecting Henry Williams to follow Beach, the trustees chose the safe candidate. Of the 71 applicants for the headmastership, Williams, at 52, was the oldest. Beach's deputy and associate for 20 years, he was not expected, nor did he attempt, to alter much in the running of the School. Restrained in manner, he was as polite as Beach had been pompous. He looked like a stopgap appointment, and, indeed, he remained at the School for only another five years, the shortest tenure of any headmaster at the School between 1865 and the present day.

These letterheads give a flavour of the type of businesses that pupils' parents were involved in. Many of them were sent as covering letters with the fees. They are preserved in the School's archive.

James Hichens, Headmaster 1895–1905. Far right: Sir Rupert Kettle, chairman of govenors, arriving at Sports Day in the 1890s.

For all that, he started to grapple with the issue which Beach had refused to face: the introduction of more science to the curriculum. For this to be achieved in anything other than a makeshift fashion, there had to be science laboratories and on that Williams ran into difficulty.

The School's finances, then as now, were finely poised, demanding cautious but imaginative management. Demands from Williams came at a sensitive time. The Great Depression had not bypassed the School. Payments on the new buildings continued. Salaries were under threat. Capitation fees had gone down. Revenue from the Rushock estate had declined to £1,899 in 1885 from £2,274 in 1882. Unfortunately, CA Newnham, standing in for the ill Kettle as chairman of the governors, told the prize day audience in 1891, 'the trustees had not an unlimited purse at their command … it would be quite impossible for the trustees themselves to do anything with the funds in the way of extending accommodation in the School'. A public appeal attracted little response. So that was that – until James Hichens arrived.

Williams recognised that he held the wrong appointment at the wrong time. The financial position continued to deteriorate and in January 1895 Williams, faced as well with what Mander called 'growing infirmity and domestic calamity', gave up so that the governors 'may have an early opportunity and a free hand to rearrange the salaries of the masters and to make other changes in order to meet the serious diminution

in the income of the School'. His successor had the same educational preoccupations: he arrived from Cheltenham College, where he had been head of science, with bold intention. 'I look forward to the time when we shall have a science department which need not fear comparison with any other school', he announced. With just six boys studying chemistry in a primitive building, he had a slender base from which to start.

Time and politics favoured Hichens more than Williams. Under Hichens the School resumed speedy development, riding a wave of compounding scholastic success in an environment of stronger public interest. Policies to take education out of its exclusive private domain, making it more generally available for all and appropriate for the naturally clever, developed in government circles. The formation of the Board of Education in 1902 as a government department signalled the state's interest.

The financial climate eased enough for funds, a mixture of private and public money, to cover the £2,000 cost of the new science buildings and library for Wolverhampton. The public money came in a £250 grant from the Town Council. This marked the beginning of an alliance between Council and School and showed the Council using powers it and other local authorities had received from central government to help the provision of education. A Wolverhampton School Board had existed since 1870 and, after the 1902 Education Act, the

Council became fully involved through the formation of a local education authority. The Wolverhampton authority would be a key player in the affairs of the School for the next 70 years.

Hichens welcomed the external involvement, publicly at least. In 1903 he told the Founder's Day audience – (Founder's Day was the new title for prizegiving celebrations and commemorated Stephen Jenyns) – that

> *Nothing but good will come from businessmen and educational experts putting their heads together and considering such questions as that of the curriculum, with the object of, if possible, bringing the School still more closely in touch with the needs of the district.*

The School, Hichens added, was ready to play its part in a coordinated system of education. He had recognised from the start that there existed in Wolverhampton a distinct demand: the School had to provide for boys going into the iron trade and so on, and it had to provide for boys going into commerce. Hence the need for the new science buildings without which 'we shall be quite unable to put before the town any satisfactory scheme of modern education'. But this did not mean turning the Grammar School into a technical school. Rather, a higher technical institution had to rest on a basis of good general education.

No previous headmaster had aligned the School so closely as Hichens with the economic needs of the town. He

established a working relationship with the Council which would last long after his departure. But this relationship would be delicate. The two were thrust together, the one anxious about the provision of education in its area and periodically ambitious for control, the other anxious for support but determined to safeguard independence. Still, they made it work until the breach of the 1970s.

In fact, the School quickly needed the Council. This was a direct result of the School's success. Under Hichens, the School roll had resumed growth and passed 200 by the turn of the century: 'we are within measurable distance of the number we can take without additional buildings', he said. There was the rub. The more popular the School became, the greater the need for more facilities. With Rushock income down to around £500 a year, additional sources of money were urgent. Help came from the government on running costs. The School had placed itself voluntarily under the control of the Board of Education and this opened the way for the government to meet the costs of up to 25 per cent of the pupils. In the jargon, Wolverhampton had become a direct grant school. But for capital investment, the School would have to look elsewhere.

As the century turned, the wish list for new buildings extended to a new science lecture room, an advanced physics laboratory and a gymnasium. At the same time the governors wanted to free the School from debt: it had taken out mortgages on the new buildings at the Compton Road site.

View of the School taken shortly before the construction of a science building in 1897. The house on the far left became the Junior School in 1911.

All of this led to a search for £2,500, as John Marston, the chairman of governors, told parents at the 1901 prizegiving. At this point the local authorities became involved. Marston himself was not only a former pupil at the School but also a Wolverhampton alderman and one of the town's great industrialists with the manufacture of the Sunbeam motor car; certainly he was ideally placed to ease the official interest. Both the Wolverhampton Council and the Staffordshire County Council promised £300 to pay off debt, Marston reported. The crucial point for the School in this arrangement was that the School and the local authorities had established a strong mutual interest, a private–public sector partnership, to safeguard development.

Probably this would not have happened had the School failed to demonstrate its academic importance. But, under Hichens, the results continued to flow. 'For the second time in the last three years we lead the way in the Cambridge senior level examination, having obtained more places in first class honours than any other school,' he announced in 1898. Four years later he declared to parents that 'the reports of all the

John Marston, chairman of governors, and one of Wolverhampton's great industrialists who started the Sunbeam brand in 1888. The company first made bicycles before moving on to motorcycles, cars and aeroplanes. The advertisement dates from 1917.

university examiners … are highly favourable – indeed, I may as well say at once, that they are, as a whole, the best we have received since I have held office as headmaster.' In 1905, *The Wulfrunian* asserted that 'the pinnacle of scholastic successes has been raised to a giddy height'.

The range of work which the results covered showed how the School had spread out from the narrow academic base of classics and catechism characteristic of its early centuries. In 1901, the range took in five languages – English, Latin, Greek, French and German – scripture, English literature, political economy, pure mathematics, mechanics, chemistry, electricity and magnetism, heat, free hand drawing, model drawing, geometrical drawing, shorthand and book keeping.

Hichens, like headmasters who came after, wanted the School to offer more than a pathway to high examination results. He encouraged intellectual growth. Under him the School gained a library, to which he donated a set of *Encyclopaedia Britannica*; the library had a thousand volumes by 1902. He believed in encouraging sport and to that end created a system of houses, based on the geographical area of the town whence the boys came, plus the boarders, and thus called North, South, East, West, School. The house system became the source of internal sports competitions and lasted, in one form or another, to the end of the 20th-century. In the interests of enhancing a sense of responsibility, he introduced School prefects. Not least, he reorganised the junior school so that it became a preparatory school for boys of eight and over and acted as a feeder for the secondary school.

Years later, *The Wulfrunian* gave a retrospective judgement. 'During the ten years of his office, the School was destined to undergo great changes and to begin to assume that form which is familiar to us now on a larger scale.' Hichens moved on to another school in Sheffield during 1905. If Beach had provided the foundations for the modern Wolverhampton Grammar School, then Hichens had built the walls.

Watson Caldecott continued where Hichens left off. Scholarship and expansion, sports and society – all continued during a period of rapid growth which brought local recognition, educational renown and the inevitable set of financial problems associated with investing for the future. Caldecott came from Trinity College, Dublin. He filled his new role at the School to the manner born. EH (Dickie) Dance, who joined the staff in 1920, described how Caldecott

Watson Caldecott, Headmaster 1905–23, and his wife. Caldecott was highly academic and a keen sportsman.

walked about the streets of Wolverhampton in a silk hat and tail (not frock) coat, and he wore a tail coat even in school. The only exception was when he went to see the Wolves, in which case he wore a brown bowler and brown tails. Stupendously handsome … he dressed the part of the great headmaster in the Victorian tradition.

Caldecott was a classical scholar. Indeed, *The Wulfrunian* claimed that he was responsible for Wolverhampton being 'one of the few great schools where the classical tradition shines still undimmed', and that 'nowhere has the head's presence been more felt than on playing fields'. He was a talented sportsman with a reputation enhanced by time and legend; it is true that he played soccer with Tottenham Hotspur, but only once, in 1894, and that without distinction: the club, then amateur, found his performance 'not impressive' and did not take him on. But he encouraged his pupils to participate and the results showed his success.

At his first Founder's Day report, Caldecott reported that 'the year had rolled by pleasantly, profitably, peacefully'. That may have been true inside the School but it was not the case outside. Little had changed in the bleak urban environment. Barnsby, an historian of labour movement in the Midlands, divided the period between 1900 and 1914: depression and mass unemployment from 1903 to 1909 and after that full employment. Applicants for relief from the Wolverhampton Distress Committee tripled in the three years to 1909. But the local economy had begun to change around the turn of the century as cycle and motor manufacture spread to complement the traditional metal industries like lock making. In more general terms, the economy recovered from the Great Depression in the years leading to World War I.

Economic recovery was a background factor in the growth of the School during half of the 18 years of Caldecott's tenure. *The Wulfrunian* claimed that 'his headmastership has been distinguished by greater general prosperity than the School has at any time enjoyed'. When he arrived there were 160 boys (the numbers having dipped in the final years of Hichens) with eight masters, and when he left there were 560 boys and 23 masters. Yet this prosperity did not come without difficulty or sadness. At first, it looked as if Caldecott's problems had many of the same characteristics as those of Hichens.

He had not long been installed when official pressure came for an improvement in facilities: buildings must be

Plaque in Big School showing the impressive academic results achieved by boys during Caldecott's tenure.

improved and enlarged, there had to be more science buildings. As Marston conceded, it had been thought for some time that the School was not up to date on equipment. Certainly the costs could not be met from revenue. The School had been running at a loss of around £300 a year from 1903 to 1906. When the Earl of Dartmouth opened new buildings in January 1908, Marston said that the building cost £2,000 and furniture £300. For that the School had new science rooms, refurbishment of old buildings, including the provision of a common room for the masters, new space for the library and changing rooms for athletes.

Early football team, 1902–3. Eight members of the team served as officers in World War I and survived but Robert Willcok (centre, front row) refused a commission, preferring to stay with his 'pals'. He was killed at Delville Wood on the Somme in 1916.

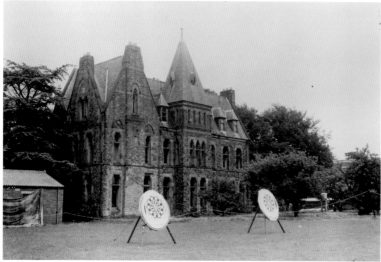

'Riddles' was converted to become the Junior School in 1911.

appealed to the governors. After the bickering, Staffordshire agreed to a capital grant of £600 and a readjustment of charges on the security of the School's estate, repayable over 30 years. Wolverhampton provided a grant of £300 a year from which the School would provide 25 free scholarships to boys from the town's elementary schools. Similarly Staffordshire provided £150 a year.

At one level, this expansion showed the School continuing in much the same way as it had done for the previous 30 years. Similarly, the 1911 purchase of five acres of land and a house, which became the junior school and which extended the School's frontage on Compton Road, conveyed the same impression. Internally too the variety of school life gained added richness in sports and societies: the School's orchestra gave its first concert; Alfred Robinson, the long-serving classics master,

This would not have taken place without the help of the Wolverhampton and Staffordshire Councils. But it was not easy. Wolverhampton wanted to gain control of the School in exchange for funds and that was not an arrangement which

Alfred Robinson joined the School as a classics master in 1890 and became second master in 1896. He wrote the school song, Carmen Wulfrunense, *and retired in 1928.*

wrote the School song, *Carmen Wulfrunense*; the photographic society had its first meeting while the natural history society became the scientific and mathematical society; a boxing club started and had to restrict membership.

But at another and deeper level, the normal tenor of school management and activity in and out of the classroom had a disturbing undertone. The tension in Europe, which burst into World War I during 1914, crept into the School

around 1911. The debating society could still find time to discuss the hoary old topic of classical versus modern education, but it sought to come to terms with contemporary worries like 'the weakness of Britain's defences renders her liable to invasion' and 'a system of compulsory military service is necessary for the welfare of this country' (lost, incidentally, by 23 votes to 17). But more importantly, because it took the tension away from rhetoric and into flannel uniforms and

The OTC at Brocton Camp, 1917. Stanley Brookes can be seen on the far right with Norman Brook, the future Lord Normanbrook next to him.

The OTC taking part in the Mayor's parade in the 1920s. JB Harding, the commanding officer, is at the back on the left.

weaponry, was the establishment of the Officer Training Corps (OTC) in 1911.

By the summer nearly 50 boys had joined, and a contingent of 20 cadets with a sergeant instructor and an officer had represented the School at a review, by the King, of the national OTC in Windsor Great Park. *The Wulfrunian*

reported the event in minute detail and, editorially, adopted a preaching, patriotic tone about OTC membership:

> *Let those who do not belong remember that they owe it as a duty to their School and country to join: they will have no need to be ashamed of joining a corps which has in so short a time reached a high standard of efficiency.*

To that, *The Wulfrunian* added a letter from Field Marshal Lord Roberts, the military hero, who spelled out 'the great necessity there is for every able-bodied man being trained to defend his country in time of need'. After the war had started, *The Wulfrunian* was angry with 'the dozen or so fellows in the upper forms of the School, who fail to join the Corps. We urge them to make good their delinquency at the earliest opportunity'. Later, the magazine observed the 'glorious response' to Roberts's appeal, asserting that the rally of former pupils to the colours 'is in no small measure due to the establishment of the Wolverhampton School OTC four years ago'.

By December 1914, nearly 200 former pupils were in the forces. By the last year of the war, the total had risen to nearly 600; to put that in perspective, the figure is double the number of boys on the School roll in the last year of peace. Their service spread across all the arms, some were officers,

The two memorial panels list the following names:

Left panel:
R. LEWIS
L. LITTLEHALES
N. LLOYD PATTON
J. A. LOVATT
N. R. LOWDER
W. N. LOWE
F. L. MALET
W. S. MATHIE
A. W. S. MOLINEAUX
A. W. MOORE
P. J. MORGAN
J. L. M. MORTON
H. G. MOULD
G. MURPHY
W. H. NOKES
R. PAGE
R. P. PHIPPS
H. PIPER
E. G. RICE
N. J. ROBINSON
L. G. SHAW
F. R. SILVERS M.C.
C. E. SIMS
L. A. SIMS
L. SMITH
S. P. SMITH

Right panel:
H. SUMMERS
J. R. SWALLOW
A. E. SWEETING
J. M. TATTON
R. THOM
C. S. THORNE
H. D. H. THORNE
G. P. UNDERWOOD
T. A. VOYCE
J. J. WALKER
H. WALTERS
J. WALTERS
F. M. WALTON
A. F. WARNER
D. S. WEBB
E. A. WEST
W. H. WHEATCROFT
H. WHITEHOUSE
N. B. WILKES
G. E. WILKINSON
F. N. WILLCOCK
R. C. WILLCOCK
A. WINTER
J. F. YEATMAN

The War Memorial Screen in Big School was erected in 1922. It lists the names of 102 old boys who died.

some remained in the ranks. Including teachers and non-academic staff, 105 died.

The dead are remembered by a board of honour in Big School, erected in 1922. It is, as *The Wulfrunian* described it, 'in stout oak in the form of a screen of the Jacobean period', 33 feet long and 13 feet high, and peers out still when the School assembles. Subscriptions from former pupils made the memorial possible.

The installation served to emphasise the growing importance of the Old Wulfrunians Association as a solid support for the School. Former pupils had started to gather at occasional dinners during the 1890s, but a formal association did not start until 1906. Subsequently it grew and spread its activities to a range of sports teams, well known then and now both at the School and in the town. Old Wulfrunian activity during the war helped the School. The need for new facilities did not diminish as the roll increased to record levels and Old Wulfrunians helped by making a gift to the School of a new gymnasium, opened in 1915. This was a practical celebration of the School's 400th anniversary which, because of the war, demanded 'that all manifestations of pomp and rioting must give way to the quietest of ceremonial', as the School's magazine put it.

On the face of it School life went on much as before. Caldecott reported on Founder's Day in 1918 the results of the Cambridge University examinations with the comment that 'there is every reason to feel proud of the continued and ever-growing success of the Wolverhampton Grammar School'. The debating society continued to discuss the rival merits of classical and modern education. Minutes of staff meetings show a normal preoccupation with the running of the School:

All of the members of this team served in the war. Two died and two were disabled. The headmaster, Watson Caldecott is standing at the back on the right.

The gymnasium was opened in 1915. Shown here is the commemorative trowel used by John Marston when he laid the foundation stone.

duration of classroom periods, lunch hour duties, standards of discipline and so on. But there were nonetheless indications that war was having an effect.

On the sports side, the School suspended cross-country running because of food shortages. More importantly, over the longer run, the war placed strain on the staff as masters joined the forces and substitutes had to be found. Indeed, Norman Brook, a pupil at the time and one of the most distinguished Old Wulfrunians as secretary to the cabinet and director general of the BBC during the 1960s, later recalled that the main responsibility for sustaining the School rested on five men: Caldecott, of course, 'a great headmaster and a great gentleman'; Francis Crickmay, the second master and in effect the deputy head; Alfred Robinson, the sixth form classics master; Jakob Fuoss, who taught modern languages; and Ernest Clodd, 'a splendid old eccentric', who ran the junior school.

Towards the end of the war, the situation at the School deteriorated. The worldwide influenza epidemic arrived. In Britain there were around 230,000 deaths, starting in Glasgow during May 1918; worldwide the death toll was 70 million. Wolverhampton could not remain unaffected.

The ravages of the prevailing epidemic were not apparent until the term [autumn 1918] was a month old: there then began to appear gaps which increased rapidly until some units almost disappeared. Not least among the suffering forms was the Sixth and prefects were as scarce as butter.

So it was reported by *The Wulfrunian*, which, in the same edition, carried an article by 'GHT', a prefect, who related how he had been called in to teach a middle school form: the epidemic had reduced the size of the class from 30 to 12.

Although the School soon returned to normal working, conditions by the standards of later in the century remained relatively primitive, as AT Rowney found:

When I joined WGS in 1919 I was put into Remove A (scholarship students), which was a wooden ex-war department army hut; a second hut housed Remove B for paying students. Cast iron stoves heated these. A supply of coke in a bucket was in each hut and a garden type of watering can was adjacent to keep filled a square cast iron tray on the top of each stove to keep the atmosphere moist. Mr Clodd used to pass these huts on the Merridale Lane every lunchtime and he used to make quite sure there were no boys ensconced within the huts and locked the doors. These were then unlocked by one of the prefects at 2.00pm.

Facilities had been steadily improved since the 1875 move but one-class-to-one-classroom did not always apply, as Dance recalled as he conjured up conditions in Big School during the early 1920s.

In my early days it was the busiest part of the building. It began, as always, with prayers. In those days the masters sat in pitch pine kneeling pews flanking the fireplaces. At that time the centre of Big School was not, as now, the platform end. There was no platform until about 1925. Before that there was an enormous pitch pine desk for the headmaster in the recess. In 1875 this desk was by the window; the recess was then the head's classroom … In those days (till 1923) the main part of Big School was occupied by two other classes.

The new science buildings from before the war had started to match up functions to specific spaces but it was not until 1920 that mathematics received its own classroom. This split the sixth form mathematicians off from the classicists, the two groups from which sprang the School's early academic reputation.

The years after the war were difficult as the national economy went into recession. The hardship spread into the staffroom, resulting in a call from teachers to the governors for a proper pay scale. Basic salaries were controlled nationally, but by 1920 the Wolverhampton masters wanted their salaries to be on a London scale, claiming that living costs in Wolverhampton were as high as those in the capital. Two years later, far from obtaining an increase, they suffered, like their peers, a reduction.

The economic difficulties forced the School's governors to examine their finances. Funds from the Rushock endowment had diminished. At the Lion Hotel, Kidderminster, the historic link of the School to Worcestershire land snapped. The estate went on to the market and sold for a gross £25,030, allowing the governors to invest in securities which might provide a better return than land. The date was 17 June 1920. Rushock had helped the School for 408 years.

Caldecott could not stay to deal with the effects of recession and recovery. In early 1923, he stunned governors, staff and pupils by resigning because of ill health. Dance said that Caldecott wore himself out: he carried on without even a typewriter, all the School's correspondence he did by hand; he consented to have a telephone but only where he could not hear it. He consolidated the changes of Hichens and developed the School into one of the leading institutions of its type, anxious not only about formal education but also about the broader preparation for life. He was, said an unnamed Old Wulfrunian, a scholar, athlete, officer and man of affairs.

Portrait of Watson Caldecott painted on his retirement.

Overleaf: Concert in Big School

3 | Warren Derry: The Booth Preamble, Peace, War and Control (1923–56)

Walter Booth came to Wolverhampton from Wellington College, Berkshire, in 1923. A Cambridge graduate who had studied both natural science and history, he was a war veteran with service in the Royal Air Force. In retrospect, his spell at the School looks like an interval between the lengthy tenures of Watson Caldecott and Warren Derry. Booth himself, when he left to become headmaster of Dulwich College, wrote to Francis Crickmay, the chairman of the staff room, 'I have had the happiest five years of my life here'. Certainly he left his mark, although, inevitably, that could not be as deeply etched as those of Caldecott and Derry.

He was a man who drew respect. *The Wulfrunian* observed that 'from the first moment he stepped quietly into the Big School it was clear that his was a personality to dominate the whole School: he was recognised by the boys as "he-that-must-be-obeyed"'. The magazine classified his time as 'an era of order and discipline'. To be sure, he had a strong sense of his own position, shown in an ugly little squabble with the staff about an annotation of one of his notices in the staff common room. The staff was 'aggrieved by the censure of the headmaster' but ended up expressing 'desire to respect the headmaster's dignity and prerogative' and inviting him to the 1925 staff Christmas dinner as a gesture of goodwill.

The other side of Booth's notion of hierarchy was a policy of pushing authority downwards. Contrary to the policy of Caldecott, who had no truck with giving the School's prefects any disciplinary powers, Booth developed the system. This he considered his greatest contribution to the evolution of the School. He gave the prefects power of punishment and entrusted to them discipline outside the classroom. His aim was to foster leadership by training the prefects to render service and train themselves in the process. Few at the time would have disagreed with the motive, even though, as staff preoccupations with discipline indicated, they might have queried the method.

Walter Booth, Headmaster from 1923–28.

Opposite page: Schoolboys in front of the School wearing new caps, introduced as an award for merit by Booth.

Clockwise from top left: Old Boys cricket, 1928; School House team in the tug of war at Sports Day, 1927; Football team, 1924–5 and a sports journal.

He followed Caldecott, however, in nurturing academic prowess. He extended English language teaching and created a modern languages sixth form. The School's tally of open scholarships to the English universities grew larger: during Booth's time there were 24, compared with 27 in the Caldecott years, when academic work had been dislocated by the war. He was at one with Caldecott in trying to make the School a community and the range of extracurricular activity spread outwards as first aid, philatelic and travellers clubs started.

Booth encouraged drama to the extent that he guaranteed £40 to underwrite what was deemed by the staff as 'an unqualified success': the first performance of the staff's new dramatic society, Oscar Wilde's *The Importance of Being Earnest*. He also created an open-air theatre in the grounds, or, rather, he had the boys dig it out for him. This venture was not a success: modern legend has it that only one performance took place there as wind rustled leaves in the nearby trees and nobody could hear the actors.

Compared with the years before and after, physical development of the School during the second half of the 1920s

was limited. Numbers had settled at around 500, which the governors thought a maximum and Booth does not seem to have pressed for an extensive building programme. Old Wulfrunians financed the purchase of 1.5 acres of more land, which extended the playing fields, and the Mander family, members of which were Old Wulfrunians, governors and benefactors, paid for the construction of fives courts. Booth himself initiated a School embellishment fund for the purchase of extra amenities.

Booth's successor, Warren Derry, became one of the giants in the history of Wolverhampton Grammar School. He came with the conviction that the School could be one of the best in the country and, in the words of Deirdre Linton, the former School librarian and Latin teacher, 'he led the School to new heights of academic success with determination'. Yet his appointment must have been a gamble: he was only 29 when, arriving from Edinburgh Academy, he took up his post in January 1929. From the outset he came across in public as austere and cool. But, as Old Wulfrunians testify, he had the innate qualities of the gifted teacher: kindness and care for the individual. *The Wulfrunian* commented that he followed the

'stern rule' of Booth but that he was 'no less firm and sure'. Of course, he had to be, as the young man in control of a group of men whose experience was considerably greater than his own.

From the start, his presence demanded deference. Allan Cholmondeley, who later became a headmaster himself, arrived at the School two terms after Derry and over 50 years later remembered how

I crept in timidly as a new red-capped boy into Remove A … The memory of my feelings about the new headmaster is one of awe … Nor was this awe confined to school

Members of the OTC at Mytchett Camp, 1927.

57

boys; it was shared even by the members of the committee which appointed him … He had a simple, broadly ecumenical, faith that cut through the complexities of intellectualism to establish a firm Christian idealism.

Derry had a clear idea of schoolmastering, telling parents in his first Founder's Day report of 'the paramount duty of trying to discover the precise channel by which a boy's mental energy can find free and productive expression' and laying down that 'a boy should feel that the School is not just an institution he attends, but a body of which he is a member'. This theme of the wider purpose of education cropped up repeatedly in Derry's pronouncements over the years. Commenting on the record results which the School had achieved in 1930, he acknowledged that School Certificate was a necessary passport to the professions, advanced education and employment generally but, he went on, 'I deplore the idea that the School Certificate should be the goal of education'. It should be a hurdle, a minimum not a maximum requirement, he argued.

How the boys of the School had been using that passport in the years between 1923 and 1930 became evident in a survey, published by *The Wulfrunian*. It showed – and the percentages are approximate – that 19.7 per cent went into offices, 17.1 per cent into engineering, 12.9 per cent to the universities, 7.3 per cent to work with their father, 6.9 per cent into banking, 6.4 per cent into farming, 4.3 per cent each to teaching and accountancy and the rest scattered into law, stockbroking, civil service, the military and local government. It is possible to read into those figures the calculation that at least a half of Wulfrunians in that era remained in the Wolverhampton area and this, of course, provided, through the Old Wulfrunians Association, a local source of support which could be – and was – called on from time to time. Wolverhampton at this time had a population moving towards 140,000 and a wide range of industry based on vehicles and traditional metalworking, so that Old Wulfrunians could be absorbed into the regional economy.

Old Wulfrunian support became most evident when School finances became stretched. In fact, in the early 1930s, the governors felt in a strong enough position to reduce their annual grant application to the local authorities, not that this should be taken as a precedent, they hastened to explain: 'it was made purely as a contribution to the present urgent need for economy'. The application in 1932 reduced to £600 from £800 for Wolverhampton and to £300 from £400 for Staffordshire. These were difficult years nationally, in the wake of the Wall Street Crash and in the midst of the Great Depression when the Labour and National Governments tightened the economy

in line with the prevailing pre-Keynesian orthodoxy. The effect 'was most devastating in education', wrote AJP Taylor in his celebrated *English History* in 1965. Even as late as 1933, the School's teachers, who had been obliged to take a 10 per cent pay cut, pleaded for its restoration, but, as it turned out they were two years premature. During this period, however, the School's finances remained broadly in balance. Receipts in 1931–2 were £17,641 and expenditure £17,311 while in the following years both receipts and expenditure were lower at £16,772 and £16,639 respectively.

Acting against the trend of retrenchment, the School had resumed the extension and modernisation of its buildings, with the construction of a new building just inside and running parallel with the Merridale Lane boundary. From 1930, this provided facilities Derry's predecessors could only have dreamed about: laboratory, workshop, library, art room and form rooms. It was, as *The Wulfrunian* pointed out, the antithesis of the old huts where boys like AT Rowney had begun their school careers. The School abandoned these huts but they

must remind scores of old boys of old times, when the ink froze, when the huts occasionally caught fire, when some fool let the fire out, when they roasted chestnuts on

the pipe, or when they involuntarily underwent Turkish baths in the summer.

The School did not forget the past and sought to anchor tradition by the replacement of the collapsed original window in Big School by the installation of a new one which showed the coats of arms of benefactors: the founders – Jenyns,

The Merridale Building was opened in 1930. It brought valuable extra facilities including a science laboratory, workshop and art room.

59

JOHN MORETON | MERCHANT TAYLORS | Sir STEPHEN JENYNS Kt | Sir THOMAS OFFLEY Kt | JOHN NE

LAWLEY T. SMITH | Sir RUPERT A KETTLE Kt | JOHN MARSTON | JOHN T. HOMER C.B.E. | GERALD

Detail from the large stained-glass window in Big School that was restored in the 1930s to include the coats of arms of the School's main benefactors.

Nechells and Offley; Merchant Taylors'; John Moreton, who provided a playing field; Lawley Smith, who gave learning scholarships; and generous chairmen of governors – Rupert Kettle, John Marston and John Homer who was the incumbent in the early 1930s.

All this building and decorative activity did not isolate the School from conditions outside. The number of boys which had hovered around 550–60 dropped. Derry told the 1933 Founder's Day audience that the current roll was 517, 'rather below average for the last four years'. He shrugged that off: the governors thought that 500, given the available accommodation, was the full complement; the decline 'is to be attributed in part perhaps to the general financial depression';

certainly it could be attributed in part 'to a slight raising of the standard required for admission'.

Derry, in other words, had more faith in his judgement of what he required of the boys than in his assessment of the financial depression. On the first point, he saw in the traditions and ethos of the School a value of work and learning, 'willingness for the standard to be set by those who wish to learn instead of those who are willing to idle'. He found that the Wolverhampton boy had 'staying power', he did not win a scholarship and then fade out. He saw 'the bent of the School' as 'towards simplicity and sincerity and modesty'. He remained anxious, however – and this he voiced a year later – that boys should not simply concentrate

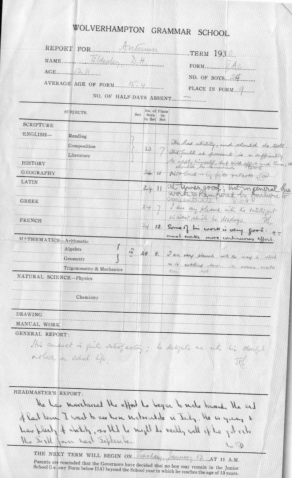

on examinations; nothing helps the average boy more, he contended, than to share fully in the life of school. Sometimes, he suggested, the parent is at fault by not encouraging it.

Certainly, during the 1930s, extracurricular activity branched out. What seems to have been the first School trip abroad went to Switzerland, followed in later years by visits to Heidelberg and Biarritz. Attendance at the Travellers Club, reported *The Wulfrunian* in 1932, never fell below a hundred. There was, the magazine noted, 'a great increase' in membership of the Scientific Society and the Debating Society while the Boxing Club, Choral Society and Philatelic Society, though not exactly flourishing, 'still clung tenaciously to their existence'. A troop of Boy Scouts started in 1930 and the OTC continued with annual camps as the centrepiece of existence. JD Swallow, a saxophone-playing pupil, started an unofficial dance band which rapidly obtained local engagements. A new system of football came into force: boys could play under compulsion or voluntarily at the wish of their parents, the majority of whom opted for compulsion.

Derry might have been able to gloss over the effects of the economic situation in 1933, but by 1935 the position of the School had deteriorated to the point where the governors expected a deficit and looked to the local authorities for help in addressing it. They asked the Staffordshire County Council for a delay in repaying the principal of the 1908 30-year loan and a reduction in the interest rate. For 1935–6, the School requested from Staffordshire a grant of £650 and £900 for the following years. From Wolverhampton it requested £1,300 for 1935–6

Top left: Taming of the Shrew, *1938; Boy's report from 1930; Below: Running team, 1930.*

Five former members of the School's OTC who joined the Staffordshire Yeomanry at the start of World War II.

By this time, worries about the situation in Europe had begun to darken the background to a decade of steady achievement. The School's debating society discussed whether isolation would best ensure peace for the British Empire; it decided it would not. The War Office had told the governors to enhance the security of the OTC's armoury with bars on the windows and an iron-gridded door. It was not long before *The Wulfrunian* told its readers of the 'patent duty to learn to serve immediately' in a repeat of its injunctions before World War I. But the School's life went on regardless as David Coast, reminiscing in 2000, described:

> *In 1937 we had little idea of what was going on in Europe. For one thing we were all kept so busy – two hours or more homework each night – Scouts every Wednesday afternoon and Friday evening, soccer, sports or cricket (compulsory) on Saturday afternoon, following school in the morning then two parades of 'the Corps' [OTC] partially in and out of school hours. At that time there were no current affairs periods in the syllabus to keep us in touch with the world outside.*

and for the following years £1,800. The School received what it wanted in 1935–6, but the demand for 1936–7 was scaled down slightly. The governors meanwhile, in the face of higher costs and lower receipts, raised the fees.

The governors also addressed the question of the boarding house, the Tower (the centrepiece of the original 19th-century buildings), observing that the number of boarding pupils had been declining steadily and that 'the time might come when the continued use of it would not be justified'. School House in 1933 could muster only 15 members. Derry agreed with that assessment, considering that the accommodation had become unsuitable for either boys or masters. The deadline for closure was put at 31 March 1937, putting an end to a practice which started in the 16th century when the lodging of boarders was seen as an extra source of income for the master and the usher.

With school children across the country, WGS boys took part in the 'Dig for Victory' campaign. They grew food in the school grounds and participated in harvest camps at Evesham.

By this time, Derry, of course, was well ensconced. He could point to academic success and, indeed, at Founder's Day, 1935, he talked of 'memorable success in the field of scholarship'. This was a reference to the record number of open scholarships to Oxford and Cambridge – seven – frequently used at that time as a yardstick of academic prowess. For the previous ten years the number had floated between two and six. Derry also talked of a record percentage of boys leaving with School Certificate: 72 per cent compared with 48 per cent, an abnormally low total for the School, recorded in his first year.

But the world outside had started to intrude and it would push Derry's tenure at Wolverhampton into a second phase. The demands of World War II on the School proved more taxing than those of World War I, in the sense that staff and boys had to participate more fully. But it happened step-by-step; war crept up on the School. *The Wulfrunian* pleaded for more boys to join the OTC (it reached record strength of 178 in 1939). There were articles in the last days of peace about assembling gas masks, evacuation from London and reports of the Scientific Society's talk on air raid precautions. But in March 1939 the magazine could still report that 'no major crises have interrupted the even tenor of this term' and it was not until eight months later that the issue of war impinged on the meetings of the staff common room. Then, prompted by the departure of Lt Roy Holmes, the staff agreed that the chairman should write a letter of good wishes to any member called to active service.

DIG FOR VICTORY

The School's Air Training Corps band in 1943.

The most obvious sign in the early years was the construction of ten air raid shelters, classified by David Coast, then 15, as excellent:

Built along the Merridale end of the playing fields, they all had sumps, regularly pumped out by the groundsman (who permitted the occasional cigarette to be smoked down in his boiler room!). With repeated practice we all became very slick in getting out of our form rooms, along the corridors, down the stairs and across to the shelters – all at a fast walking pace. Gas masks were carried at all times and no running was allowed.

Once war had started in earnest, coping with it became more time-consuming. Meeting the injunctions of the national Grow More Food campaign, boys of the fifth and sixth forms cleared the ground for two allotments next door to the ill-fated open-air theatre. Boys were sent back to the land, joining camps in Evesham at harvest time to bring out the fruit and vegetables, at which they became quite expert: 88 tons of plums, 36 tons of apples and 100,000 plants of Brussels sprouts in 1942. The staff became firewatchers, slightly grudgingly it appeared from the common room minutes, stating a willingness 'if governors judged it necessary and no other means of doing the job could

be found'. Some masters found it difficult to stay awake all night; it seemed better to plan the rota so that a master firewatched for one half night in four rather than one whole night in eight.

Everybody had to cope with inconvenience, petty and serious. As *The Wulfrunian* observed in 1942, 'the last year of the war has taught this magazine, like the School itself, to make a habit of uncertainty'. Transport was restricted after school hours. After two years of war, the staff noticed a shortage of board rubbers and ink. The School's railings disappeared, required as scrap metal for the war effort. Food rationing teased teenage appetites. Mowing the sports grounds was not done as frequently because of a shortage of petrol, but then, as Alan Rogers, who went to the School in 1940, remembered:

There was little opportunity for sports. Although inter-house competition continued, all matches against other schools had been suspended. A few chess matches were arranged and as a junior member of the School team I recall one unusual match against the Municipal Grammar School. It was in early 1942 on a day when

Eric Markham OW (pictured) was killed in World War II during training. Shown here is the telegram to his mother announcing his death and a letter of condolence from Buckingham Palace.

Robert James Boyd OW served as a Spitfire pilot. He survived being shot down over the Channel in 1941 but died in 1943 when shot down over France.

we awoke to see a particularly heavy snowfall. I was unable to ride my bike through the 15 inches of snow that covered the streets. The town's buses were not running. So I walked more than two miles to School where Bennett, the School's maintenance chap, was busily clearing pathways between buildings. Following classes

we played our chess match, winning a majority of the boards. I walked home. By then it was dark and late as perhaps 7 o'clock.

Still, the School was spared the worst. Derry, on the first wartime celebration of Founder's Day in October 1943, reported that 'so far the School has been exempt from the severe hardships, and in some cases, tragic experiences, which not a few English schools have encountered'. It had not been bombed. Derry anyway told how the 'older schoolboy of today takes his school work and pre-service training in his stride', referring to work in civil defence, the Post Office and on the land. But this assessment looked designed to reassure.

In fact, even apart from coping with physical difficulties, the School worked under considerable strain. By 1944, the roll had climbed to 583, greater than at any time in the past. This represented an increase of nearly 20 per cent over the maximum number the governors in peacetime had thought the School could handle and resulted directly from more boys remaining after they had reached 16 and swelling the size of the sixth form. Indeed, the School did not have enough desks to go round. But what might in more ordinary times have been a cause of satisfaction, now raised the question of how the boys would be taught. As early as 1941, *The Wulfrunian* reported that staff turnover was 'more than usual'. Later, higher turnover merged with shortages. This had one marked effect.

The Memorial Grounds at Castlecroft were bought in 1949 by the Old Wulfrunians Association to commemorate the war.

Detail from the memorial in Big School to those who died in World War II.

Necessity cracked the male bastion: women teachers arrived. The first formal recorded presence of a woman on the staff came in the Red Book, the School's lists of staff and students, of October 1942. There are the names of Miss C Edelman and Mrs M Barnshaw. And the first mention of a woman teacher in the minutes of the staff common room appeared on 23 November 1942.

Notwithstanding the changes, School life went on. Boys sat down to School Certificate. Musical activity increased with the arrival of Frank Rust. Derry's dominance remained unchallenged. 'He lived behind the dreaded green baize door (off the main hall of Big School) through which offenders passed for caning. Not that this was a frequent occurrence', David Coast recalled. But the thought of it frightened, or amused, younger boys, not least RW Riley of Remove A who brought Tennyson to his aid:

> *Into the room of pain*
> *Strode the sixth formers,*
> *Canes to the right of them,*

One of a pair of stained glass windows given by the School's founder, Sir Stephen Jenyns, to the church of St Andrew Undershaft in London. The windows were sent to WGS before the war for safekeeping and Gerard Mander arranged for the School to keep them. They hang now in Big School.

Boxing team, 1945.

Canes to the left of them,
Canes at the back of them,
Volley'd and thundered,
Storm'd at with swishing cane,
Boldly they bore the pain,
'Till out of the room again,
Came the sixth formers.

When the war ended, *The Wulfrunian* gave a sigh of satisfaction in its first peacetime editorial:

The School is healthy and vital. It has come soundly through the war. Morale is as high as ever. Relaxation of disciplinary influences has brought no corresponding deterioration. School standards, academically and athletically, are the same.

But, of course, the war could not be swept away quite so easily. Over 600 Old Wulfrunians went to war, more than in the conflict of 1914–8, and 69 former students, teachers and non-academic staff died. The youngest was 19 and the oldest 50. But this toll was lower than in the first war. However, one who returned was Roy Holmes, the first member of staff to go to war and who later became deputy headmaster.

Even before the end of the war, both Gerald Mander, chairman of the governors since 1934, and his colleagues, and Derry and his staff started to come to terms with a fundamental change of status for the School. They could do this in the knowledge that in parliamentary debates on the future of education, during 1944, the School had been classified as one of the four best grammar schools in the country. It was a measure of the changes which had taken place over six decades.

Government austerity and fiscal tightness during the inter-war years had stultified any major changes in the national system of education and schools like Wolverhampton, by and large, had been been left to their own devices. All of that changed with the Butler Education Act of 1944. In general, it decreed free secondary education for all. In particular, it split the school population into three as a result of a competitive examination at the age of 11, what became the dreaded 11-plus. Bright children would go into grammar schools, about 15 per cent of the school population, less bright children into secondary modern schools and those with a technical bent into technical schools. The question for Wolverhampton Grammar School was how it would be funded and who would control it.

Mander and the governors, Derry and the staff, would have preferred to maintain the prewar status, classified as direct grant. The government provided a percentage of funds to pay for some pupils and the balance of funding came from what the School organised: its own investment income, fees paid by parents, some help from the local authorities and a limited number of privately endowed scholarships. The School ran its own affairs.

In the new situation, the School had four possibilities. It could shrug off involvement with the authorities and become completely independent; it could surrender independence to the local authority; it could continue as a direct grant institution; or it could apply to be what was called voluntary aided.

The first route would be difficult to sustain without a much larger endowment than the School had. The second looked unattractive given over 400 years of independent running. Mander reported on Founder's Day 1945 that the government had rejected the application to remain as a direct grant school, without providing any reasons, so that ruled out the third route. Later it became apparent that Wolverhampton did not fulfil the government's administrative criteria for direct grant status; the *Midland Counties Express* explained that although the Minister of Education retained a direct grant list, the status would be given mainly to schools receiving pupils from several local authority areas. This did not apply to Wolverhampton which had a catchment area of the town and south Staffordshire.

The School, then, had been pushed back to seeking voluntary aided status. This would mean sheltering under the local authority umbrella but maintaining self-government. The

local authority would select the pupils and support the School financially, but in return for its measure of independence, the School would meet half the cost of buildings and maintenance. Failure to meet the financial obligation would lead to the School going into local authority control. Governance would be somewhat clumsy with, in effect, two boards: one for the trust and endowment of the School as a charity, the other for the School as such, on which there would be substantial local authority representation.

Top: The Travellers' Club resumed trips abroad in 1949. Members of the Club are shown here visiting the Palace of Versailles. Bottom: The Scientific Society visiting the Hardy Spicer propeller factory in 1950.

Senior boys in front of the Merridale Building, 1950. Far right: the classical sixth form and staff, 1953.

In fact, obtaining voluntary aided status proved a close run. It was done by all three parties involved, School, local authority and ministry of education making generous assumptions about the School's financial position. For the local authority, the matter depended on the timing of building alterations, given that the School's investments (not taking into account a recent sharp fall in the price of gilt-edged securities) and sinking fund came to £30,016. But if building works took place in the near future that sum would be wiped out as the work would cost £60,000. 'Everything', said a memorandum from the Wolverhampton borough treasurer's department, 'seems to turn on whether the alterations can be deferred until 1965 or after. If not, it is doubtful whether aided status will be conceded.' The ministry of education took the view, without any strong basis of calculation, it appeared, that the School could accumulate £16,000 of reserves over the coming years and that should see it through. But, as HBC Horrell of the ministry's legal branch told the governors, the minister took the decision to grant aided status 'with some hesitation', urging the governors at the same time to let the headmaster's house and junior school building.

But the main point was that he took the decision. The School opened its doors to the bright young boys of Wolverhampton and south Staffordshire. For the first time, its education would be free. Derry now entered the crowning years of his career, little changed in manner but holding all the strings of power. 'It was a silver period for the School and it was a very good school in those immediate postwar years', commented Tony Stocks who joined the staff as a

24-year-old history teacher and, at the peak of his career more than 20 years later returned as headmaster. 'Derry collected a very good staff, quite a number of whom became heads themselves. He ran the School with one secretary and he did the appointment of staff all on his own.' The School was in his image, and it was conservative in conduct and curriculum.

Derry was largely interested in classics and mathematics, like his 19th-century forebears. He did not recognise history as a sixth form subject until about the time Stocks started. In his last years, responding to the national need, he opened up science teaching. John Darby, who joined as Derry left and, indeed, was interviewed by him – 'very formal, not unpleasant' – found no biology master and one other chemistry master. The winning of Oxford and Cambridge scholarships was his great pride: 125 of them during his tenure.

Although Derry was at home with ideals of mass education, he chafed at interference from those he saw as misguided authorities. He used to make his attitude clear in Founder's Days speeches, as in 1947:

This School is a very sensible School, doing quite a lot of things quite well … We do not attempt more than we think we can carry through successfully, we do not share the belief so common today that schools can and ought to do everything; and we do not feverishly revise out the whole curriculum every time the bees buzz more loudly than usual in the bonnets of the educational experts … We should not hide our heads in shame if anyone called us old-fashioned, and we would even confess to thinking that quite often old things are good, and good partly because they are old.

He had a humorous side which was not always apparent, but which has become the basis of the legion of stories still exchanged in Wulfrunian circles. Robin Cooper, whose schooldays finished the same day as Derry retired, related to

The WGS choir, conducted by Frank Rust, made a recording of 'Golden Slumbers'.

69

An intrepid scout abseiling down the tower, 1951. Boarders were accommodated in the tower until boarding came to an end in 1937.

The Wulfrunian how one day Derry 'approached Jeff Till, the cricket master, who was carrying a newborn baby in his arms. Derry stopped, looked closely, then said in a sepulchral voice, "Not bad for the first attempt".' In another incident, caught by Stocks, a boy fainted at one of Rust's concerts, causing Derry to leave his seat, showing his caring attitude, and mutter to Stocks at the back of the hall, 'Thank God something's happened. It's a duet. I hate duets'.

School concerts provided one small piece of evidence of a School which had rapidly resumed normal working after the war and the changes brought about by the 1944 Education Act. The house system changed in 1947, dividing the School into six; from 1897 to 1936 there had been five, and from 1936 four. The new houses adopted the names of benefactors – Homer, Jenyns, Marston, Moreton, Nechells, Offley – and the idea was to create more internal competition in both sports and other activities. That same year the first party of Wulfrunians since the war went to Paris and drama productions resumed. The military side of the School, now named the Combined Cadet Force continued, going onto Cannock Chase for exercises twice a term with blank ammunition. 'It would not be forgotten', BM Leek recalled in *The Wulfrunian*, 'that a frequent operation was held in which the party was split into two halves representing attack and defence'. School life had become so stable that, for the first time in his Wolverhampton career, Derry noted that there had been no staff changes in 1951.

Masters worried about discipline and noise but had to acknowledge that their supervision was often inadequate, prompting William Carhart, then chairman of the staff common room, to record in the minutes that a large measure of responsibility lay with the staff: 'we must tackle the matter ourselves if we were to justify the privileged position held by the School'. But these worries do not seem to have interfered with academic success. As the old School Certificate gave way to the General Certificate of Education, Derry said, 'our results taken altogether, are the best there have been'. By 1953 he could claim that the number of boys going to university had doubled since 1939. By this time the School had skewed round to enlarge the sixth form at the expense of younger boys. The preparatory department stopped taking boys immediately after the war. Total numbers at the School drifted down from the wartime highs to around 520, but 20 per cent of those were in

the sixth form by the early 1950s; this constituted a doubling of numbers compared with the pre-war years.

All of this meant that when Derry retired in 1956, the School had a high reputation both nationally and locally. Its weakness was its buildings, as the Ministry of Education pointed out in a report which asked if the School was using what it had to the best advantage. This threw up the perennial problem of more science laboratories and the limitations of Big School as a point of assembly. Nevertheless, for the bright boys of Wolverhampton it was the place to be.

But the man who had watched, helped and encouraged Derry for the greater part of his Wolverhampton career did not live to see its end. Gerald Mander had become a governor in 1914 and chairman in 1934. Antiquarian and historian of the School and Wolverhampton, member of a wealthy industrial family and benefactor, he could not have been more closely linked to the School. He died in 1951. When given his own portrait during the closing months of his life, he remarked wryly that 'this is one of the few presentations where I have not been asked to subscribe'. Those subscriptions were extensive: he provided a common room for the staff, he had fives courts built, he helped the Old Wulfrunians Association fund a World War II memorial window in Big School and the purchase of the Castlecroft sports ground.

Playboy of the Western World, 1950.

Warren Derry, Headmaster 1929–56.

Overleaf: Students on the front lawn, 2010.

4 | THE UNEVEN ROAD TO INDEPENDENCE (1956–78)

Ernest Taylor came to Wolverhampton in September 1956 from the headship at Quarry Ridge School, Liverpool. The successor to Warren Derry was a historian and, like his predecessor, he would place importance on scholastic achievement, even more so perhaps. 'The School stood for scholarship under him', observed Robert Brandon, a historian himself, who Taylor recruited to the staff. 'He was an academic through and through.' John Darby, who was Taylor's first appointment, classified him as 'a kindly father figure who changed the whole atmosphere of the School'.

Quickly after his arrival, Taylor wrote to the parents, stating that the change in headmasters 'will not involve any change in the real direction of the School's progress'. At that point, this looked a reasonable aspiration. The School was secure in the educational organisation of borough and county and it had a national reputation. The town itself, while not the prettiest,

Opposite page: The visit of HM Queen Elizabeth II in 1962 marked the highlight of the School's 450th anniversary celebrations.

Ernest Taylor, Headmaster 1956–73.

had grown to a population of around 140,000 and had an economic life which, based on the vehicle industry, looked prosperous enough to draw immigrants. Ten years later, the future looked uncertain and maintenance of the status quo did not look an unquestioned option.

Internally, Taylor had three aims, he told the parents. He wanted boys to have a sense of belonging in the School's community, he wanted honest work and good character alongside consideration for others, and he wanted no false distinctions of pride and diffidence between boys and masters, the clever and the less so, the athlete and the rabbit at games. In other words, he sought a community more at ease with itself than would have been possible under an autocracy like that of Derry's. In retrospect, it is possible to see, in the tone Taylor tried to set, a bridge in mood and approach between the sternness of his predecessor and the more freewheeling attitudes of his successors. If Derry represented the 19th century carried over into the 20th, Taylor was emphatically of his time.

This became quickly apparent. He grasped the issue of science teaching where Derry had only fumbled. Darby talked of 'explosive growth' and 'the start of a big expansion' so that by the early 1960s, he had six boys in the science sixth trying for scholarships at Oxford and Cambridge – five won them. Taylor introduced biology, 'against the wishes of the heads of department', according to staff common-room minutes, for the sixth form and the top science sets in the fourth and fifth forms. By 1957 there were 42 boys in the science sixth and 35 in the mathematics sixth, together more than those studying classical and modern languages. But the expansion created its own problems.

HM Queen Elizabeth II being greeted by the Headmaster, Ernest Taylor.

Visit of

HER MAJESTY

QUEEN ELIZABETH II

WOLVERHAMPTON
GRAMMAR SCHOOL

THURSDAY 24th MAY 1962

On Founder's Day in 1957, Taylor explained that the sixth form science and mathematics absorbed all the time of the science specialists, all available teaching space and prevented the extension of science to boys not specialising in it. So the School needed new buildings and new staff if science was 'to become a respectable part in every boy's education'. The need for new facilities exposed the School's financial frailty, given its obligation, if it wished to retain its voluntary aided status, of finding half the cost. The state of the economy did not help: high inflation, high interest rates, a decline in the value of its securities and increase in costs. So the School went out to appeal, seeking £50,000 by 1962.

The parents rallied round with 98 per cent of those having a boy at the School agreeing to give £1 a term. The Old Wulfrunians Association did its part. Corporate Wolverhampton fell in behind the School with donations from many of the great names of British and local industry and commerce. Together they safeguarded both the expansion plan and the School's independence. By 1960, the physical facilities of the School had been transformed with the remodelling and expansion of rooms and laboratories for science, new dining hall with a stage, and changing accommodation for sports. This followed the early step of Taylor's tenure, taking over the headmaster's house to extend the School's space adjacent to Big School. The headmaster had a house on the opposite side of Compton Road. The School now wanted a new building for the junior school.

So, by the time of the School's 450th anniversary in 1962, science had been boosted, finance had been secured and expansion had been put in place. Taylor had made a quick impact. With a clean-up and a paint-up, the School stood ready for a visit by the Queen to help the celebration. But the School found that in its voluntary aided state it could not always build when it wanted. It had to wait for approvals from the ministry of education in London and this did not necessarily arrive when the School desired. So the final stage of Taylor's programme, the removal and replacement of the junior school, did not take place until 1969.

The Derry Building housing the new dining hall and classrooms was opened in 1960. It was named after the previous headmaster, Warren Derry.

The junior school building was an old Victorian house, purchased with its grounds in 1911 as the culmination of that generation's expansion programme. Taylor condemned it 'as ugly as it was academically unsuitable'. In his report at the Founder's Day celebration of 1969 he acknowledged that the old building had been unsafe for years (even the demolition contractors did not dare work on the dry rot-riddled top floor). Its disappearance coincided with the completion of the Hallmark building, named after Henry Hallmark, a generous and devoted chairman of the governors, with new form rooms, a music room and gymnasium.

School numbers had been rising again during the earlier part of the decade, eventually passing 600, nearly a third

of whom would be in the sixth form. There the balance of specialities split roughly even between science and humanities. 'The old dream of a grammar school providing a continuous course to the sixth form is becoming a reality here', said Taylor in 1963. Half of every annual intake of about 90 boys went on to a university and 80 per cent of boys continued to GCE A level.

In those days, free of the demands of the national curriculum, teachers had considerable autonomy. 'We didn't use textbooks much when I started', Robert Brandon recalled. He taught history as a series of problems which could be discussed and resolved. 'The tendency under Taylor was to appoint good people and let them get on with it.' For the

The Junior School was demolished in 1969. The Hallmark building was completed in the same year.

Left: Sixth formers, 1960s. Below: Marine Biology trip in the 1960s. Taylor put a great emphasis on expanding science teaching and introduced biology to the curriculum.

on Saturdays. In classrooms, the boys sat in rows and were addressed by their surnames. During the early 1960s, the boys had a working week of 5.5 days, made up of 37 periods. (Saturday morning school attendance stopped in 1968.) This number made it possible for all of them to cover arts and science subjects up to GCE O level; once they reached the sixth form they chose either two arts subjects and one science, or two science and one arts.

The social side of life at the School, the extracurricular activity, waxed and waned. Sports remained strong, but that had become a habit of achievement. Music drew in more and more boys with large-scale choral performances. A brass band started in 1965; it grew out of the concert and jazz bands, explained Florence Darby, who was on the music staff at the time, to such effect that, at its concerts, people had to stand in the hall. Societies, however, had an uneven existence. *The Wulfrunian* listed 15, running from Boy Scouts to chess to scientific in 1963, but a year later was reporting a meeting which looked at the causes of their decline and found myriad problems: failure of committees, apathy, self interest, too many of them and too few members, lack of time, shyness … The response was to bundle the societies into an overarching society, the Sir Stephen Jenyns. Two years after that, Taylor talked to the Founder's Day audience of 'the great recrudescence of house activity in games, hobbies, music and drama'. Yet, in 1968, *The Wulfrunian* had to complain about a bad year for the Jenyns and suggested that what had been bundled up should be unbundled. During 1971, the magazine reported, the Apathy Society emerged and, by definition, faded away.

Mr Powers conducting the School's brass band.

young Brandon, the heads of department seemed 'titans'. Especially in the second half of Taylor's headmastership, they appeared to operate as 'baronies', as Gareth Phillips put it; he was another Taylor appointment, as a chemistry master.

Life in the classroom was not free and easy. Masters held positions of respect, sometimes enhanced by the application of the slipper to the ears of the recalcitrant learner. Failure to complete homework, or, in some cases not to complete it up to standard, led to detentions, held after school hours or

Left: Queen's Scouts, 1955.

Below: Scout troop at Goatfell Summit, 1950s.

Lack of interest led to the demise of the Combined Cadet Force. John Appleby, who was at the School from 1955 to 1962, remembered that

> *the CCF loomed large over the life of the School and I joined at the age of 12. Wednesday evenings were devoted to cleaning and ironing kit and Thursday afternoons mainly to square bashing. Light relief was provided by field days which largely consisted of getting hopelessly lost on Cannock Chase.*

By 1959, the school management committee of the Wolverhampton Council was, according to a resolution,

> *regretting that the Combined Cadet Force is still a prominent feature of the curriculum of the WGS and express the hope that it will be made clear to parents that joining of the CCF is wholly voluntary.*

In fact, the CCF atrophied and in 1971 was formally closed down.

Painting of front of school with The Pebble in front. The Pebble, sculpted by Glynn Williams (OW 1950–5) won the Gulbenkian Award and was given to the School in 1962.

By this time, Taylor was in the closing years of his headmastership, marked not only by the completion of the building plan but also by the recognition that the future of the School in its shape as a traditional grammar, acting independently but with public support, could not be assured. These years denied Taylor's early promise of continuity, not so much in what went on inside the School as in how it responded to what went on outside where the political pendulum swung towards and away from the Labour party.

Wolverhampton and other grammar schools found themselves in an anomalous position. They were the butt of criticism for those believing that education should not depend on selection, but they remained a goal for many families wanting the best opportunities for their children. The historian WN Medlicott explained that, between 1945 and 1963, 2,397 secondary schools had been built but that dissatisfaction with the system built up in the face of the nervous strain involved in having a child's educational future decided by the 11-plus examination. Those who passed went to grammar schools, those who failed went to secondary modern schools, seen as a settling tank for academic failures, wrote Nicholas Timmins in his history of the welfare state. Was the system democratic? asked Medlicott. The rigid division between those selected and those not created unnecessary tension and fear among parents and children, asserted Brian Lapping in his history of the 1960s Labour government. The Labour party, which regained power in 1964, was alert to the feeling. It ran neatly in parallel with its own ideology, the search for equality.

For Taylor, as a champion of grammar schools, the arguments remained clear-cut and he articulated them in speeches to parents, Old Wulfrunians and professional bodies like the Association of Voluntary Aided Schools. He made the speeches from a position of considerable strength, both because the School itself could be seen as successful but also because he had won personal respect for his intellect and concern for standards in and outside the educational world. 'I remain unconvinced that any new overall pattern can safeguard the twin aims of education in depth and general education', he said, rejecting any one-size-fits-all outcome for the educational system. He was 'against the oncoming wave of egalitarianism and uniformity in secondary education'. Grammar schools had a triple line of defence: their legal status, springing from the 1944 Education Act (and in the Wolverhampton case spelt out

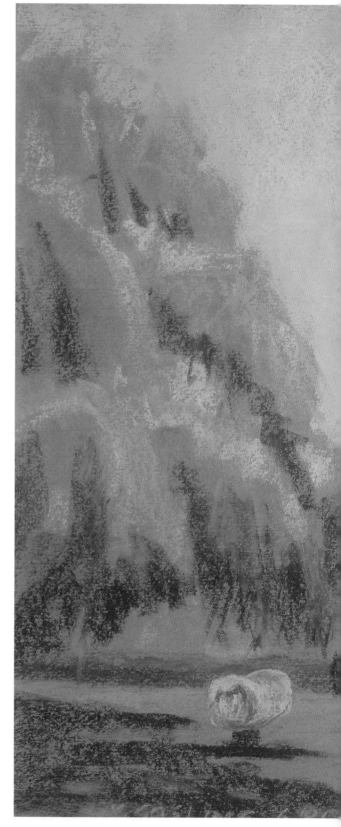

Wolves players celebrating their FA Cup victory against Blackburn Rovers in 1960. The cup was later put on show at at WGS as part of a School event.

in the articles of government no. 166, sealed on 13 July 1951); the fact that they provided options for parental choice; and their maintenance of high academic standards.

The government, while determined through Anthony Crosland, the secretary of state for education, to work towards a single comprehensive system of education, could not act directly. At that time, central government had no legal responsibility for providing schools; that was in the hands of the local authorities. So Crosland in 1965 sent them a circular asking for a scheme which would reorganise schools on comprehensive lines, that is without selection based on the 11-plus. Voluntary aided schools should be included in the scheme. A year later, Crosland followed that up with another circular, this time with a sting. It made clear that only new building consistent with the development of comprehensive reorganisation would obtain official approval.

The School, then, would have to deal with Wolverhampton Council, with which it had been in generally amiable relations since taking voluntary aided status. Taylor believed that the local authority would resolve to preserve the contribution the School made to the boys of the town, but he could not be sure. He told a dinner of Old Wulfrunians in 1967 that, without reassurance from either the Council or the ministry, the School had three choices.

The first would be acceptance of defeat, as he put it, and become a comprehensive secondary school; this would probably lead to a loss of reputation and of distinguished teachers. Second, it could leave the public sector and become independent, as some Old Wulfrunians had urged, although

the School's reputation had been built up by educating boys whose parents could not afford fees; certainly it would need more financial support than had been forthcoming from recent appeals. Third, it could negotiate with the local authority and on that, he said, nothing had been settled, not name, not size, not method of recruitment and not the purpose of education.

The Wolverhampton Education Committee produced its plan for reorganisation in January 1968. It envisaged comprehensive development at the pace of building programmes. It defined three categories, immediate, short term and long term, with the short term likely to extend over ten years. The last schools to phase out selection would be Wolverhampton Grammar School and Wolverhampton Girls' High School; both would go into the third, long term, phase of the scheme 'for subsequent review'. If that left open the date of the Council's decision on its intended relationship with the School, it looked as if there would be, at any rate, a breathing space of ten years.

Whatever reservations he may have had in private, Taylor in public presented the plan optimistically, as a support for the School. Grammar schools might be under critical fire, he told the Founder's Day audience in 1970, but 'it is encouraging to know that our local education authority continues to have confidence in this School'. A year later, he took an even more roseate view: the role of grammar schools was to care for the needs of the academic minority at the top of the intelligence range, he said. 'This has become our role locally and the local authority's reorganisation plan has been in line with this thinking in its plan for our place in Wolverhampton's educational provision'. Acknowledging the courage of the policy, he added that it made it possible to attract and pay more highly qualified heads of department.

There the matter rested but not for as long as Taylor expected, as his successor found out. Taylor's activities in support of grammar schools gave him a high profile in education circles and he became increasingly in demand as a public speaker. This came on top of his duties as a Methodist lay preacher. All of this led to the suggestion that his attention to the detail of the School was not, in the later years, as assiduous as in the earlier years. Connie Brough became Taylor's secretary for the last two terms of his tenure (and stayed to work with another three headmasters). 'I didn't see a lot of him. The School seemed to run itself. He'd be going two or three times a week to the station, to go to London for meetings. And he spent a lot of time in Ludlow preparing his house (for retirement).' Roy Holmes, the second master, ran the School, 'from the back of an envelope', Darby said. 'Cover for absent staff he'd work out in assembly and you could hear Holmes stage whisper at the back of the School. It was a bit ad hoc', Gareth Phillips commented.

Ernest Taylor retired at Easter 1973. Henry Hallmark, who had been chairman of governors, retired two years earlier than that because of illness and his successor, Philip Mander, who, like Gerald Mander, came from the Wolverhampton industrial family, died soon after his appointment. But he had time to choose Tony Stocks to follow Taylor and in doing so he kept the position in the family, as it were. Stocks was the headmaster at Sir Thomas Rich's School, Gloucester, but he had begun his career at Wolverhampton where, for ten years, he had been a highly respected history master and an outdoor enthusiast, running, for example, the Boy Scouts.

Tony Stocks headed the School for five years, arguably the most tumultuous in its history, not only because decisions had to be taken about its future but also because of the conditions in the national and local community.

He arrived in the year when oil exporters curtailed international economic growth by sharp increases in their prices and stricter control of their production. Their moves came at a time when politics in the UK had become more rancorous, when labour relations had become increasingly turbulent; they simply exacerbated an already difficult set of economic and social circumstances. Europeans and Americans labelled the UK of the early and mid-1970s as 'the sick man of Europe' and it was true that, during that period, separate factors merged to handicap the economy: sloppy management, recalcitrant trades unions, lack of investment, rising inflation to hit an annual rate of 26.9 per cent in August 1975. The Labour party returned to power in 1974 and brought with it the education policy, defined during the previous decade, which Taylor had opposed and which looked inimical to the School's interests.

Of all the major issues of social policy in the seventies, wrote the social historian Arthur Marwick, 'education engendered most controversy'. Although there had been debate and dispute about broad social and professional issues like techniques of teaching and levels of freedom for pupils, the flashpoint of controversy was independent schools and

Tony Stocks,
Headmaster 1973–8.

selection. The tone and firmness of Labour's approach became clear during its years of opposition. Roy Hattersley, in a speech to teachers on 8 September 1973, set out the intention:

> *I must, above all else, leave you with no doubts about our serious intention initially to reduce and eventually to abolish private education in this country. The pursuit of equality of opportunity has to be replaced by the pursuit of equality itself.*

He argued that comprehensive and selective education are incompatible; the 11-plus examination should be abolished; it was no use of taxpayers' money to purchase places in selective independent schools. Given the existence of a Labour council in Wolverhampton, it looked likely that the 'subsequent review' of the status of the School, foreshadowed in 1968, would be sooner rather than later.

Practically, in any case, it seemed that Council interest in the School had diminished. David Lambourne, who joined Stocks in January 1974 as one of two deputy headmasters (the other being Victor Hartree), thought 'the Council had withdrawn in spirit'. He noticed that there had been little capital or maintenance expenditure. The School had no photocopier. It was so badly equipped that a television set had to be hired from the town to see the election results of February

1974. By this time Stocks detected what he would later call 'sharpening knives' at the Council as he noted the presence of some councillors who were no friends of the School. At best, the governors and Stocks together had to deal with a rather detached partner. This was one problem for Stocks. But he also felt that he worked in a shaky environment. There has been too much change, he told parents in 1975:

> *The continuing reorganisation of secondary education, the recent reorganisation of local government, the proposed changes in the examination at 16-plus, which envisages a common O and CSE level by 1981, the threatened reorganisation of other exams and examination boards, the shortage of teachers in certain vital subjects, the shortage of cash for vital capital expenditure, the threat of serious cuts affecting many facets of school life, and the general lack of direction in contemporary society are all threatening the stability of the teaching scene and creating a lack of confidence within the profession.*

Stocks, in short, had to undertake his educational housekeeping against an uncertain background and with no assurance of continuity. He made changes. Like incoming headmasters before and after him, he felt the School needed 'freshening up'. Looking back to those years during his retirement, he remembered how he found

> *a lot of staff had been there a long time with not much experience of other schools. Taylor had given a lot of authority to heads of department. There had been little opportunity to appoint new staff and the School needed an injection of new staff from other schools and other disciplines. There was a departmental fixation.*

One example of that was the small size of a central library: the departments had created their own. Indeed, PJ Aggleton of the science sixth had complained to *The Wulfrunian* in 1970 of the uncontrolled development of separate libraries with little or no coordination between them.

Old Library in the Merridale Building, 1978.

Opposite page: Students making the most of the sixth form library.

Clockwise from top left: Geography room; At work in a science laboratory, 1978; English lesson in Derry Building.

David Lambourne saw the School as being in a rut. 'Taylor was fixated on Oxbridge', he remembered. 'There was a tendency for the better staff to be allocated to that end. Stocks wanted that dealt with, he wanted to improve the quality of teaching.' Stocks wasted no time in passing on the message. 'I remember Stocks at his first staff meeting saying the School reputation was that it was very good for very able pupils: there was a need to be helpful to the less endowed academically,' Brandon recalled. Except for mathematics, academic streaming was abolished, there being no point in it with an intake of a narrow range of abilities. The curriculum was remodelled to provide a greater number of subject choices in the higher forms. Stocks introduced a school council where form representatives could discuss improvements in non-academic affairs.

With facilities still falling short as numbers tended to increase, the School needed another building programme: more sixth form accommodation, a new library, a leisure centre, a second biology laboratory, a place for instrumental teaching and more specialist rooms. In the troubled 1970s, writing such a shopping list was wishful thinking. Yet, in spite of the physical weaknesses and the uncertainty about the future, School numbers continued to rise, reaching 647 in 1975.

Contacts between the governors and the Council about the future had been made in 1974 and Denis Grayson, the director of education, had started to draft a document dealing with the School's future status. At Founder's Day that year, Stocks dealt with what he saw as the threat to the School's existence. This followed a further circular from the government, pushing the comprehensive programme. The future of grammar schools had become a political issue and if this circular went into effect, Stocks said,

There will be no free selective academically based school to serve this population of 300,000, whereas certain other authorities and areas will continue to be served by at least a hundred of the present direct grant grammar schools.

'Is the accident of history which prevented the School from being direct grant years ago to determine what happens to Wolverhampton ablest boys?' he asked. The answer from the Council corridors appeared to be 'Yes'.

In the first recorded discussion by the staff about the future of the School, Keith Brockless made the point that the School could not hope to escape attention. The discussion did not go far; the staff wanted to be kept informed by the headmaster about the position of the governors, but, as Lambourne told the meeting, the governors could scarcely have an attitude until the exact form of the legislation affecting the School was known. This, of course, remained an obstacle. There was little firm on which negotiators could chew except the one basic point that selection would have to go if the School remained inside the state system.

Malcolm Ward, a distinguished Old Wulfrunian who joined the governors in 1972, remembered the talks as being like 'a game of chess'. Meetings between a sub-committee of the Council's education committee and a sub-committee of the governors were 'polite but hanging over them the possibility of a leak to the press from Labour councillors'. The aim was to find a modus vivendi, how to live between a system which ruled out selection and a system which thrived on it. Probably the task would have been impossible anyway. Ideas like turning the grammar school into a specialist music school floated through the negotiations, but to no effect: 'they didn't want to find a bridge', Ward said.

Going into 1977, the position remained vague. Stocks reported to the staff that in many respects he knew as little as they did; the policy of the governors was to hold fire until the local authority had drawn up its scheme. The Council had made one proposal which required spending of £750,000 on building, 15 per cent of which would be met by the governors, but Stocks had the impression the proposal came 'with less than complete seriousness'. The School would be accepting another selected intake in September 1977 but after that the position remained opened. By the autumn the future remained unclear but the temperature had risen.

Hallmark gym, 1970s.

Stocks, in another report to the staff, said Council representatives had visited the department of education in London and been reminded that, under its articles of government, the School was entitled to select the most able boys who opt to go there. If the Council abolished selection tests, the governors would have to consider instituting selective tests of their own. This put the gulf between School and Council in a legal framework. The possibility of a final breach, with the School becoming wholly independent, had become the stuff of staff discussion.

Meanwhile, rumours circulated, reported in the local press, of the School's imminent demise. On 11 October 1977, under the headline 'Grammar Faces A Slow Death', the Wolverhampton *Express & Star* published a report, with lengthy quotations from Councillor John Bird, the leader of the Council, that left few doubts given that, as Ward suggested, 'he was in command; he was used to getting his own way'.

If they [the School] wish to remain in the state system they will have to conform with the conditions for comprehensive education. Otherwise they will have to go independent and find their own money ... I think it would cost them at least £1m. We need the places we already have at the School ... We have poured money into it. If it goes independent this would all have to be paid back to the taxpayer ... On top of that the School would have to find all the money for staffing. At the moment they have difficulty finding the money for repairs ... We have held talks with the governors at great lengths, but there is still a wide difference of opinion. I cannot see an amicable settlement coming about ...

Assembly in Big School.

Opposite page: Leavers with the traditional final day messages on their shirts.

Nor did it on the major issues. Still, the severance of the formal links was low key. 'Council workers came down one afternoon in a van, pinned a notice on the front door and went away again', Connie Brough remembered. The notice reflected the substance of a report from the education committee to the

full Council of 2 November 1977. It declared the intention to cease to maintain the School and not to allocate pupils to the School in September 1979 and thereafter. It referred to the 1976 Education Act eliminating selective admissions, drew attention to the Council's long-term plans set out in 1968 and the failure to reach a mutually acceptable plan with the School's governors. The Council would continue to pay for the education of pupils presently at the School.

Oddly, Parkfields Comprehensive School in Wolverhampton gave the Council the stimulus to act when it did. There had been structural damage at this school that had caused the Council quickly to move in some temporary mobile classrooms. The Council thus discovered it could accommodate boys in other schools who would otherwise have gone to the Grammar School without immediately engaging in a costly building programme.

The amicable side of the settlement was informal. The Council originally had intended to stop the allocation of boys to the School in September 1978. Tony Stocks and Denis Grayson had been friendly for years. John Bird, other councillors and members of the Council staff had boys who had been or were at the School. These contacts, the informal network, were instrumental in giving the School a breathing space of a year.

The governors responded quickly and declared for independence. Members of the Council on the board conveniently stayed away as they took the formal decision. Stocks took the matter philosophically, as the *Express & Star* reported in February 1978:

You couldn't expect a local Labour authority to go against their central government. It was a perfectly reasonable thing to do however harsh it appears ... There is a place in society for a school like this. Look anywhere in the town to see how business and professional life is stacked with Old Wulfrunians. Don't they want the same to happen in future?

The School would now find that the decision to become independent, to hold on to the tenets of academic and social belief, to move outside the cosy confines of local authority maintenance, was easy in comparison with making a pathway in the noisy outside world.

5 | STRIKING OUT ALONE: STOCKS INTRODUCES THE HUTTON YEARS (1978–90)

As 1978 dawned, the road ahead looked perilous for John Roper, the chairman of governors, and his colleagues, and for Tony Stocks, the headmaster, and his colleagues. They had undertaken to create a whole new infrastructure for the School. At one level this was a liberation: free of local authority control they could organise affairs in the way they wanted. At another level, they had to face the fact that they had little means of using that liberation and the time they had to find the means was limited. Roughly they had 18 months to create a financial base, to find the means, until the summer of 1979. But it had to be obvious that this was possible by the end of 1978, around the time when parents would be considering whether or not to seek admission for their boys, the first intake of the new independent School.

The School, though, had tangible assets. It owned its land and buildings; indeed, its resources had been swollen by a recent legacy from Henry Hallmark: he left the whole of his home to the School, recalled Connie Brough, the headmaster's secretary. 'The music hut was full of his stuff; people were buying things like solid silver and the money was going back into school funds. His chairs were in the staff common room until they wore out.' Malcolm Ward, the Old Wulfrunian judge who became chairman of governors after Roper, remembered that 'at independence we had government stocks

A stained glass panel in Big School remembers Henry Hallmark's generous legacy.

Opposite page: Pupils using the entrance named after John Roper, chairman of governors.

worth about £25,000'. So there was security for any future borrowing, in which, of course, the School had not had to engage for over 40 years.

At the same time, the School had intangible and unmeasured assets. This was the repository of goodwill which could be translated into financial support. Over the years the School's boys had spread out into the professional and commercial life of Wolverhampton, while the Old Wulfrunians Association had a wider geographical spread.

Stocks and the governors launched an appeal. Their aim was to attract £700,000, two-thirds of which would provide bursaries for boys from families on low incomes, an attempt to hold the grammar school ethos of providing top-class education to the bright, regardless of background. The other third would go on new buildings, the need for which had become pressing.

'I already had some expertise in fundraising', Ward related, 'so when the time came I said to Roper, "I'll look after the appeal, you have enough to do." Dennis Norton, a governor and businessman – he became chairman of the industrial side of the appeal. And corporate Wolverhampton rallied round.' The parents of boys at the School rallied round too. Stocks went out to the public: 'it helped to have been in Wolverhampton before [he had been there in 1947–57]; a lot of people in Wolverhampton knew me – Old Wulfrunians and so on – and my successor continued that'. Appeal notices went out in the local and regional press. The School engaged Craigmyles,

Discussions during 1978–9 covered areas like the cost of the Council maintaining boys at the School, that is to say, the boys who were there already and those who would come in September 1978. They involved the amount the School could spend under existing capitation schemes and how those schemes would fade out. There were haggles about when and how the Council's contribution to School repairs would be paid in the period before formal independence. On the other side, valuations had to be placed on the equipment which the School would take over and buy from the Council, large like the language laboratory, small like individual desks. For the School's bursar, Alan Martin, the process demanded skill and infinite patience.

In the first years of independence, the Council remained the main source of income, but, as the boys financed by the Council left the School, that contribution would fade away. After seven years it would disappear. It had to be replaced, in effect, by the money coming in from fees because income from the School's early endowment and that derived from the invested proceeds of the appeal would never offset more than a minor part of the School's expenditure. The School set the fees for the first year of the independent intake at £320 a term, broadly in line with the rates charged by independent day schools nationwide.

The appeal, the disentanglement from the Council and the arrangement of future income showed the School adapting to the private sector, becoming, in fact, more like a business. The books would have to balance, although, registered as a charity, the School eschewed profit. Instead of sheltering under

professional fundraisers. It worked. Money came in and reached the appeal target within a year. This proved to be the most successful appeal ever run by a school up to that time.

The appeal did not on its own clinch the financial future of the School. There was another element. The School and the Council had to disentangle an association which went back to the days of the 1944 Butler Education Act. This proved a complicated and sometimes tetchy negotiation. Councillor John Bird had been slightly wide of the mark when he said the School would have to pay back all of the Council's investment over the years, but there were areas where the Council had a claim on the School. For its part, the School wanted to hang on to Council money as long as it could.

an official umbrella, it had to take responsibility for its own overheads and capital investment; it had to conduct its own labour relations; it had to find its own way in the educational marketplace and do its own recruitment. All of this, however, ran in parallel to the working of the School.

For the most part, boys saw no change in everyday School life. But this was not the case for staff. As early as December 1977, the staff in a memorandum signed by John Thorpe, the chairman of the common room, and sent to the governors, called for an offer of employment 'to all existing teaching staff on terms not less favourable than they would have enjoyed had the School retained its present status'. This involved payment of salaries and the continuation of the existing superannuation scheme. The memorandum also wanted masters to have freedom to return to the employ of the local authority 'on terms not less favourable' than those enjoyed at the Grammar School.

None of this proved a great problem, but abrasive discussions did take place between representatives of masters and governors on whether staff would be able to opt for secondment from the local authority while teaching at the School. In the event, there was little change, recalled John Johnson, who at that time had been at the School for five years teaching physical education and chemistry, 'only a couple of staff went'. Indeed, for older members of staff the independent school offered a more congenial atmosphere than local authority employment. 'There was a stiff tradition – high achievers, quite old, Oxbridge, blues – and so on.'

The staff stayed but the headmaster decided to go. Tony Stocks, dealing with troubled domestic circumstances, felt that the School's new start needed a new leader, somebody younger who could set the School on its fresh footing. Roper was disappointed with the decision, Stocks remembered. Still, Stocks left in July 1978 surrounded by goodwill – 'he was absolutely on the side of the School', said Ward – and he helped in the selection of his successor. He left a considerable legacy. As a man with firm academic principles, he had kept up the School's scholastic standards, while trying to foster a greater sense of community and a spirit of what *The Wulfrunian* called 'trust and outward-looking enterprise'. He was popular, especially with the sixth form, to whose well-being he had paid much attention. He had loosened up the School after the rigidities of the Taylor years. He had guided it through some of the most troubled peacetime years of the 20th century.

Patrick Hutton, Headmaster 1978–90, oversaw the School's transition to independence in 1979.

In the late 1970s and early 1980s, as the School's position changed, there were other departures and arrivals. After the death of Philip Mander, Ernest Westwood became chairman of governors; he was very good when the challenge came from the local authority, Stocks said. John Roper was his deputy and successor and it was he who handled the transition from public to private. When he died in 1981, Ward succeeded and that set off a lengthy period of stability in the top governance of the independent School.

Patrick Hutton took over as headmaster in September 1978, giving him the final year of the School's status as voluntary aided and under the Council, alongside the task of preparing for the independence of September 1979. He undertook the tasks with swashbuckling energy.

His background appealed to the governors: education at Winchester School and St John's College, Cambridge, experience in Birmingham, so he had a feel for the Midlands, teaching inside and outside the independent sector and latterly headmaster of St Marylebone Grammar School. This last position gave him a special aura in the eyes of the governors because he had engaged in a long drawn out struggle up to the Court of Appeal with the Inner London Education Authority to keep open the School. He failed, but he had shown himself not only a doughty champion of the academic ethos of a

Grammar School to go it alone

Headmaster Mr Patrick Hutton

Ieadmaster Patrick Hutton ame to the school in September to lead the way to ndependence. A graduate in English, educated at Winhester and St John's College, Cambridge, his first eaching post was at King Edward's School, Birmingam. Before coming to Wolerhampton he was for nine ears headmaster of St farylebone Grammar chool, London. He is a ounder member of the lational Council for Educaional Standards and has ppeared in several televiion programmes concerned ith education. He says: Schools like Wolverhampon Grammar School must ontinue to stand for xcellence."

"Passing for the Grammar" is a secret ambition nearly every parent in the past has cherished for his child.

Traditionally, grammar schools have opened their doors to any clever youngster from any background; doors that will take the ambitious into the professions, management, the upper reaches of industry, commerce and the Civil Service.

Now, sadly, those doors in most towns have closed as grammar schools are engulfed in a wave of comprehensives.

Help with fees

Wolverhampton Grammar School is determined to keep the banner flying. It is transforming itself into an independent school which will maintain all the old grammar school traditions of academic excellence, hard work and a fostering of individual skills and ambitions.

From next September pupils who enter the school will have to pay fees of around £300 a term. But a generous response from past pupils and parents, friends and local industry has already built up a half-million pounds fund to provide financial assistance to those in need.

Headmaster Patrick Hutton explains: "We want to continue taking the kind of boys we have always had — boys who are curious about things, who want to find out more, who enjoy exercising more, who enjoy exercising their brains.

Competitive

"We're looking for boys of whatever race and from whatever background who will find a school of this kind exciting and stimulating. And we're offering assisted places approaching full fees to parents with low incomes.

"We don't want lack of money to stand in anyone's way. Entrance will be by competitive examination, with 75 boys being admitted at the 11-plus stage. My advice to parents is: if you've a bright boy put him for the examination, and if he seems to have the potential we want, come and discuss the money with us afterwards."

On attaining its independence the school will take pupils from any area of the West Midlands. The only geographical criterion will be the practical one of getting there by the time school starts at 8.45 am.

There are no plans to take boarders but the school may admit girls later. Besides the main entry of 75 boys at 11-plus the school will offer 15 places a year to boys of 13-plus, and also places in the sixth from.

Sixth form entrants will have to show good O-level results, usually six Os in academic subjects. Places will be dependent upon there being vacancies in chosen subjects. Parents of boys entering at 13-plus and to the VIth will not qualify for financial assistance.

The examination for first-

Wolverhampton prepares for independence

year boys will be held at the school on the morning of January 20. It will be rather like the old 11-plus exam — an English composition and comprehension test, a mathematics paper and an intelligence test.

Boys will sit the 13-plus exam three days earlier on January 17. It will include additional papers in French and science.

Parents of boys wishing to take either examination are asked to return the completed application forms as soon as possible, and not later than December 31. Results will be notified to parents before the date when most local authorities ask parents to nominate their choice of secondary school. So if a boy is unsuccessful it will not in any way affect his chances elsewhere.

Examination entry forms and all further details can be obtained from The Bursar, Wolverhampton Grammar School, Compton Road, Wolverhampton. Telephone: 21326.

Music as a part of life

Wolverhampton Grammar chool's academic eputation is coupled with nother — excellence in nusic.

About a quarter of the oys learn a musical instruent, and have the chance o play in the school's 0-strong orchestra or qually large brass band.

Both give a large number f public concerts each year nd many past pupils have one on to play professionlly. There is also a junior rchestra and a junior brass nd woodwind band.

Boys are taught by isiting teachers, with eginners in small groups ntil their musical ability an be gauged. First form oys are actively encourged to take up an instruent and their first year's uition will be subsidised.

There is a fund available o give financial help to nstrumentalists throughout he school who show paricular promise.

There is also a large horal society, at present ehearsing for a perforance of the Messiah, and a maller choir.

"We really live music ere" says a member of the nusic department staff. Everyone joins in, teachers nd boys alike."

Boys who want to do their wn musical thing get every acility and encouragement. Currently, pupils and memers of staff are running heir own Victorian ballad roup, a "barber's shop" uartet, a Christmas rock roup — and even a society or swapping punk records.

The older part of the school faces Compton Road.

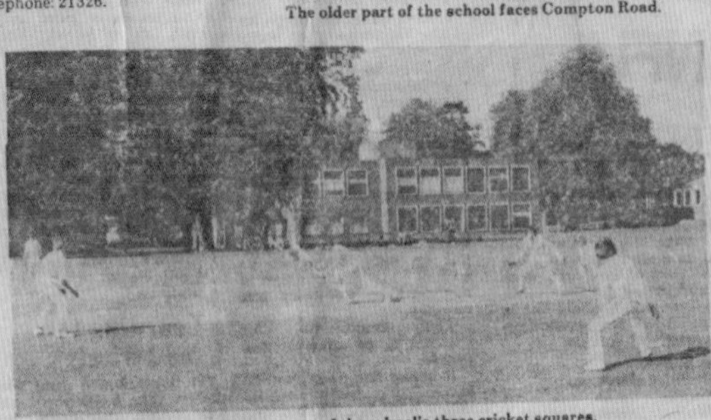

Match in progress on one of the school's three cricket squares.

Academic excellence, caring — and activities

What has Wolverhampton Grammar School to offer?

One obvious attraction is its site, almost at the town centre and easily accessible from all directions but surrounded by 20 acres of tree-ringed playing fields.

The 470-year-old school moved to its present position in 1875. Some of the buildings, including the assembly hall (known as Big School) and nine classrooms, date from that period.

But most of the other buildings, including dining hall, science blocks, gym, language laboratory and many of the classrooms, are modern. Planned for the near future are a new library complex and an additional biology laboratory.

Pass rate

As far as its academic record is concerned, Wolverhampton Grammar is one of the leading schools in the country. This year, for example, 55 out of the 75 boys in the upper sixth went on to universities and polytechnics. This included 13 entrants to Oxford and Cambridge, eight with awards.

At O-level the average number of passes per candidate was 7.3 and the subject pass rate just over 80 per cent. At A-level the pass rate was 88 per cent and boys passed in 182 out of the 207 examinations they took, with 51 passes at Grade A.

When boys join the school they are taught in three unstreamed forms that from September will have 25 boys in each. From the fourth year, when the O-level syllabus begins, classes are divided into ability sets in French and maths, but this is the only form of streaming.

The school takes the Oxford and Cambridge Board GCE examinations. Boys normally take a minimum of eight O-levels each, with a wide choice of subjects that include Greek and Russian. English, Maths, French and Science are all compulsory subjects. Boys must pass at least five subjects at grade C or better before being admitted to the sixth form.

Boys who join the school at 13-plus will stay in a form of their own for the first year.

The vast majority Grammar School boys sta on in the sixth — this ye there are 170 boys in th two sixth forms, a studying for A-levels.

Despite this intensive sy labus there is a VI for programme for gener education, in which boy can, for example, learn a additional language, take one-year O-level cours study art or musi appreciation.

By modern standards, th school is small — 620 pupil small means friendly and has always been a plac where boys treat each othe with tolerance, kindness an respect.

Staff have tended to sta at the school. Many of ther know all the boys by nam They also give their tim and interest unstintingly t after-school activities.

Much of the day-to-da running of the school done by the three senic prefects, elected by fellov sixth formers, and 23 pre fects. There's a Schoo Council of staff and boys.

The school house system i largely run by the boy themselves with fortnightl house meetings and annua inter-house contests i music, singing and game Pupils with comparativel little sports ability have chance to compete.

Experimental

After-school activitie have always flourishec Scouting is strong, with 3 boys in the Scout troop an 15 Venture Scouts — one c the largest Venture troop in the area.

Other societies include a angling club, a strong ches club, and groups for suc interests as model railway stamps and science fictior An experimental theatr group gives an almost pro fessional training i theatrical techniques.

The school has alway roused feelings of affectio and loyalty, among old boy and parents. The Ol Wulfrunians Club ha premises in Castlecrof Wolverhampton. Th Association of Friends Wolverhampton Gramma School, is a hardworkin group of parents, Old Boy and friends, who not onl arrange the annual garde party but are always pr pared to move in wit financial or practical help.

Games for everyone to play

Few schools in the West Midlands have better facilities for games than the Grammar School.

With five football pitches, three cricket squares, three tennis courts, four Fives courts and two badminton courts on the site there's every opportunity for daily practice.

It's not surprising that the school are winners or runners-up in a number of local and national competitions.

Most notable recent successes have been in cricket, where the first XI was unbeaten this summer, in Fives where two teams won the public schools Fives competition, and in badminton.

Everyone likes to be in a winning team — but what about the boys who are never going to make the first or even the second XI? Games master David Seddon has devised a far-ranging programme to encourage all boys, athletic or not, to take up some sport they can enjoy in adult life.

From the third form on pupils are given a taste of an amazingly wide range of activities which include sailing, ski-ing, golf, orienteering, ice and roller skating and ten-pin bowling.

Activity

Mr Seddon says: "When they leave school many of our boys will be working from desks. Our aim is to get them interested in some kind of physical activity they can continue when they're working.

"Winning cups is the icing on the cake but I regard this work with the 60 per cent of boys who aren't athletic as the most important part of my job."

Dates for your diary

Dec. 31, 1978. — Final date for applications for entry in September, 1979. Prospectus and registration form from The Bursar, Wolverhampton Grammar School, Compton Road, Wolverhampton. Telephone 21326.

Jan 17, 1979 — 13-plus entrance examination at school.

Jan 20 — 11-plus entrance examination at school.

March 17 — Results to parents by this date.

Ambitious boy leaders

Senior prefects Andrew Husselbee, Richard Green an Daniel Rowe shoulder a lot of responsibility for running th school. They're also ambitious in their own fields. Seventee year-old Andrew wants to study medicine at Oxfor Richard, also 17, is stydying history, English and politic studies with a view to taking a business course.

Eighteen-year-old Dani hopes to go to Cambridge study English.

But, like many other bo at the school, their abiliti don't stop at their books.

Andrew plays the violin the orchestra and plays the first XI in both footb and cricket.

Richard captains th school first XI and the tov under-nineteen XI football.

Daniel is one of th school's best singers as w as playing cricket for th first XI.

They've all enjoyed all t opportunities the school h to offer— though they say does mean a lot of ha work.

The school has a strong chess club.

Master and pupil at work in the biology laboratory.

Music is an important part of life at the school.

Brass band concert celebrating the School's independent status.

grammar school but also a man of determination. When, in 1990, Ward provided a retrospective job specification, he set out the qualities the governors sought and which they believed Hutton possessed:

> *In addition to running the School, he has to see that the business management side is set up, almost from nothing … We were looking for a man who could take all this in his stride, someone with experience and expertise as a headmaster, a toughness and ability to fight his corner when inevitable problems arose, a capacity to be the public face of an independent school in a competitive world and a hostile political climate, but with a sympathetic understanding of the ethic of this School.*

The new headmaster did not have an easy hand to play. Although the general election of May 1979 provided him with a national Conservative government which had inherent sympathy with Wolverhampton and other schools like it, by contrast the local conditions for launching a new enterprise lacked promise. Hutton took over just as the labour turbulence of the 1970s came to a peak in the

breaking up of national pay restraint agreements; he took over just before the combination of an international economic downturn and domestic fiscal tightening sent shudders through a Midlands commercial and industrial sector already under strain.

In any case, Wolverhampton's industrial base had begun to change. Local historian Chris Upton observed how, by the 1970s, the family businesses which had been the backbone of the local economy had been falling to multinational groups. As these groups reduced in size, there was a knock-on effect to small companies. Between June 1978, as Hutton prepared to arrive, and September 1981, Wolverhampton lost 18 per cent of its industrial jobs. Unemployment climbed to reach 19.8 per cent by 1985 and by then, the lowest point of the economic cycle, 25 per cent of Wolverhampton families received some form of income support – a far cry from 1961 when support went to just one per cent of families.

Nor were the local political circumstances propitious. Labour councils of the 1980s showed a degree of ideological aggression which pushed unfriendliness to the School and its ethos outside the normal courtesies, so that mayors,

Opposite page: Newspaper feature on the School's path to independence.

Mrs Lynne Johnson and pupils in the new library.

Opening the Stephen Jenyns Library, 1981. From left to right: The Master of the Merchant Tayors' Company, Mr AW Howitt; Judge M Ward, chairman of governors, Mr Hutton, headmaster and Colonel Langton, President of the Indpendence Appeal.

for example, refused to enter the School. The mayor of Wolverhampton was an ex-officio governor, who attended meetings when the Conservatives held local power. 'As soon as the Labour party was back in the majority, we were tersely informed that there was no point in inviting the mayor to our occasions', Hutton said in later years.

For his part, Hutton, while not discourteous, remained as wedded to the independent ideal as the Council was in its opposition to it. He made no secret of that as, in the early months of his headmastership, he pushed hard both to establish the new School in the town and to ensure that there would be a steady stream of applicants for its

services. Through *The Wulfrunian*, he laid down his line on comprehensive education:

> It's a fine ideal socially, but I can't agree with the methods being used to impose it. Our rulers have shown a shattering lack of concern for academic standards. The grand aim to achieve a just and equal society is having an opposite effect, because schools like this are having to go independent.

He elaborated on that in an interview with the Wolverhampton *Express & Star*:

> The comprehensive ideal is a very noble one, but in practice, in city areas particularly, it has been uniformly disastrous. It has seen the destruction of the old grammar schools which had traditionally provided children from poor homes with the opportunity to compete on level pegging with anyone from our society.

In a limited way, the School could continue to provide that opportunity with bursaries funded largely by the investment income derived from the appeal money. The School set out its offer in a full-page advertisement in the newspaper, which had Hutton saying to parents:

> We don't want lack of money to stand in anyone's way. Entrance will be by competitive examination, with 75 boys being admitted at the 11-plus stage. My advice

to parents is: if you've a bright boy, put him in for the examination, and if he seems to have the potential we want, come and discuss the money with us afterwards.

If the generous response to the appeal gave the first public reaction to independence, then the second reaction was response to the call for applicants to come to the School in September 1979. That was equally encouraging: the number of applicants exceeded the number of places available, with 132 boys taking the entrance examination for 11 year olds. 'We had been biting our nails a bit', Hutton remembered.

These two reactions signified that Hutton had a good start. The School had the chance of a new beginning and Hutton could now concentrate on running it. He had been preoccupied with the appeal – not least addressing 25 public meetings – and plans for the future, he confessed at the end of his first term. The first phase of those new plans would be the building of a new library and new biology laboratory and that would start soon, he said at the end of his second term. Then came what he called, at the final assembly of his third term, a noble moment in Wolverhampton Grammar School history.

This is the last time that we, representing as we do a fine and ancient school, will be meeting together as a state school. On September 1, Wolverhampton local education authority will be waving farewell to us, as we launch out on independence.

Hutton wasted no time in imposing his personality on the School. A big man, with a mane of blond hair and the face of a matinee idol, he had, as Connie Brough said, 'a presence about him'. Robert Brandon, the history teacher, talked of how 'he radiated mission and enthusiasm'. This had a downside, of course: Hutton himself acknowledged that sometimes he did not think through his ideas and Gareth Phillips, who taught chemistry, thought 'he had an unfortunate tendency of not admitting when he got things wrong'. John Johnson found him 'a strong character, imposing, and you didn't want to be on the wrong side of him'. Still, all who worked with and around him agreed that the School owed him a debt, that he was a good man for seeing the School along its new independent road.

Top: The Lister laboratory, named after the School's first biology teacher, was one of the first buildings to open during Hutton's headmastership. Below: The School's first computer room was situated in the present headmaster's office. It was equipped with Tandy TRS 80s.

Change came quickly. 'What a year this has been for the School!' exclaimed *The Wulfrunian* at the end of 1980:

Two years' intake are with us. Time will tell how they compare with those who have gone before. Going independent, however, has meant more than just fee-paying pupils. Our two splendid new buildings, the biology lab and the library, testify to that. All of the administration work previously done by the education authority must now be attended to ourselves and new offices have had to be created to house the bursar, his staff and the receptionist. How ever did we manage without a receptionist?

There was more to it than new offices. Hutton pushed for greater extracurricular activity and at the end of the year he could point to the establishment of the rehabilitated organ and the first organ concert, four choral and orchestral concerts, three brass band concerts, three plays, and house music and drama competitions. Independence had not dimmed the intrinsic liveliness of the School.

Classroom, 1980.

In the background, though, there was the nagging worry that the fee-paying intakes of new students would not provide high enough intellectual calibre to keep up the School's academic record. Then there was an unexpected stroke of good fortune, especially given the dire economic circumstances of the time when the government had in place a programme of cuts in spending on education. This not only removed doubts about the School's future finances in the short and medium terms but also opened the School to a wider catchment of families.

The government, over the head of opposition in the cabinet, introduced the assisted places scheme. 'With direct grant schools abolished, the aim was to replace the help they had provided to bright working class children, but subject to a means test', explained Nicholas Timmins in his history of the welfare state. It would be like a return to the conditions of financial support to which the School had been accustomed before 1944. As Malcolm Ward recalled:

There we were scraping around with a limited number of bursaries, with things threatening to be tough to provide a sensible number. Then the scheme came along. We jumped aboard so eventually we took in 40 per cent of our boys on the scheme. This was one of the highest proportions in the UK. It really did mean the School was providing for bright kids, like a traditional grammar school.

The assisted places were for pupils living in the borough, but from the School's point of view this was fine. As a voluntary aided school, boys had come from all over the borough to the Grammar and money had nothing to do with their selection. Fee-paying pupils, however, tended to come from the west and north of Wolverhampton and not from the lower-income areas to the east. On the south side, the School ran into competition with the Birmingham schools; there was little educational migration northwards.

The social mix of the School changed, of course, once entry became related to income, but the assisted places scheme altered the mix back to something akin to the era before 1979. Florence Darby, wife of John, the long-serving science teacher, and a music teacher from the days of Frank Rust, observed that the staff did not know which pupils had scholarships. Gareth Phillips said that the social mix never became noticeable in the

WGS staff in 1981.

School, illustrating the point with a recollection of how he used to run a chemistry quiz team. One evening he had dropped off a couple of boys afterwards, one to a luxurious house, the other to a deprived council house but the two had got on perfectly well out of school.

By the time the assisted places scheme had swung into effect, in 1981, Hutton had worked himself into control; any period of settling in had passed. He had begun to address internal issues like staffing and facilities. Like most incoming headmasters he wanted a mixture of change and continuity.

As far as his staff was concerned, both Brough and Ward, reminiscing, suggested that Hutton felt the School had become too staid. Brough talked of him 'weeding out'. Ward said,

'Hutton reckoned the School needed to be whipped into shape: the staff had too much independence, they were local authority employees and difficult to shift'.

At the practical level, Hutton in effect abandoned the Stocks system of delegating authority to two deputy headmasters, Victor Hartree and David Lambourne. Hartree, in any case, was ill, could not cope and became head of classics but he eventually died from a stroke. The way Hutton handled his removal from deputy headmaster upset the staff and the union became involved. Lambourne was simply sidelined into a largely administrative role, although he retained his title: 'Hutton was not a great delegator', he said. Like Stocks before him, Hutton brought in new staff and had a flair for

Certainly the staff had to respond to the new independent environment with flexibility. At first there were two senses in which they faced new demands. The first was that the School, working in an open and competitive world, had to open itself up for scrutiny, to hold open days, to host garden parties, to gather members of the new Association of Friends of the School. This could not work without the support of the staff.

The second was Hutton's pursuit of the same notion as Taylor and Stocks: the School as a community, with pupils doing things together outside the classroom, recognising that life is not just work and that the School has, as Hutton put it, 'to try to ensure that everyone cultivates forms of involvement which will maximise their chances of living interesting lives'. To this end, Hutton set aside Wednesday afternoons for all forms of activity, in the hope that what was done then might spread to hours outside the normal school working day. He put more emphasis on creating School sports teams, basking in the reflected glory of five Old Wulfrunians who, unusually, simultaneously won football blues at Oxford and Cambridge universities. Again, extended extracurricular activities could not take place without the support of the staff.

Possibly the biggest change which the staff had to face during Hutton's headmastership was the arrival of girls in the sixth form in autumn 1984. There had been discussion about co-education among the governors during the preparations for independence. A sub-committee had been set up but this decided that such a change would be too much to undertake at that time; further, the fundraisers thought a change to co-education would dilute the attraction of the appeal. The matter was left at that stage in the knowledge that the admission of girls would take place at an unspecified time in the future. So the arrival of 14 girls was the first step. The reaction outside the School was confined to some surprise that the admission had not happened sooner, although there were Old Wulfrunians who complained about a breach of tradition.

The older teachers had never taught girls, so for them even the limited scale of the co-education was a culture shock. Phillips recalled that there was a 'bit of a panic' about what would happen if a boy and a girl started an amorous relationship. That passed. And it felt better for the staff that the girls were placed in two forms rather than four. Some of the boys, Darby said, reacted against the girls with displays of arrogance but that passed too. Scholastically, staff found

WGS took its first 14 girls into the sixth form in 1984.

Opposite page: Big Six students outside the recital room, 2009.

appointing bright young teachers as heads of department: Kevin Riley in English, his own subject, and Bernard Trafford in music, for example. He created heads of the sixth form, middle and lower schools and charged them with oversight of discipline and the the range of pastoral care. John Darby – Hutton was his fourth headmaster – would later say that Hutton's dedication rubbed off on the staff, encouraging them to further effort.

Balloon Fundraising Day – part of the 1985 appeal which raised money for the School's new facilities.

Patrick Hutton, a representative from Merchant Taylors', Judge Ward and John Whitehouse.

the impact of the girls to be mixed. 'The girls who did history were not terribly good. They were not very academic or very interested. But not all departments would say that. In biology they were good from the start', commented Brandon.

But there was another sense in which the influence of the girls crept through to both staff and boys. Their presence led to a general relaxation of discipline, the cultivation of more friendly relationships between staff and pupils. Part of that sprang from the assumption that girls should be addressed by their forenames, an abandonment of the traditional formality of calling boys by their surnames. Deirdre Linton, a Latin teacher by profession but the librarian from the mid-1980s, remembered that the presence of girls improved library behaviour and their use of books was greater than that of the boys. But that has to be set against a low standard:

Being a teacher it didn't take me long to realise how the sixth form had been bullying the librarians quite disgracefully. As they seemed to be on everything, I guessed that they had been betting on how soon they could get

Above: A captain from the Army Air Corps arrives by helicopter to give a talk to the Aviation Society, 1988.

> *each librarian to leave. At the end of term, just before*
> *break one day, I asked the leading light of the betting*
> *syndicate – loudly and publicly – if he had paid out yet.*
> *He went white, and the rest of the sixth formers there for*
> *a compulsory period went deathly quiet.*

Linton worked in the new library, one of the first new buildings of the Hutton era. Alongside staffing questions, the improvement of facilities was one of the first areas Hutton felt obliged to address. Even after the start of the assisted places scheme, both he and the governors inclined to caution for fear that a change of government would stop the scheme and open up the prospect of a hole in the roll. In late 1984, with independence well established, he warned:

> *We have to husband our financial resources to enable us*
> *to face that contingency. We are therefore considerably*
> *inhibited in our thinking about the future physical*
> *development of the School. We became independent on a*
> *shoestring and while … our position is stronger now than*
> *it was, we are in no position to throw the money about.*

For all that, he changed the fabric of the School. He presided over a sustained programme of building, making up some of the shortcomings which became apparent during the days of Council control. After the library, with its cruciform shape and its amalgamation of the scattering of smaller departmental libraries, and the new biology laboratory, came projects for a

HRH the Duchess of Kent visited the School to officially open the John Roper Room.

103

A class in the IT suite, 1988.

Opposite page: Big Sixers get to grips with map reading, 2010.

The new sixth form common room, now the head's study, 1988.

sports hall, proper rooms for the sixth form, and a craft, design and technology facility to take in the small woodwork shop and little computer room.

To bring them to fruition, the School went out to appeal for a second time, seeking £500,000. This proved too much to ask but enough funds came in to undertake the projects with the exception of the sports hall – that would come later. Meanwhile the governors acquired two vacant houses adjacent to the School's site on Compton Road and they provided new suites of classrooms. The Friends financed the construction of a gallery in Big School, enabling the whole School to be seated together for the first time and the conversion of space around the assembly area into common rooms.

Hutton realised a transformation in the School and the building programme was the concomitant of the change in status. The School was his monument. When he retired in 1990, Malcolm Ward could say:

> *He has handed over to his successor a school in great heart, in as good a shape as it has ever been, and I believe a happy place. For if his duties were carried out with professional skill, and vision, and vigour, they were also carried out with good humour.*

It was a good professional epitaph.

6 | BREAKING WITH THE PAST: THE TRAFFORD YEARS (1990–2008)

One summer evening in 1990, the School's heads of department gathered to meet the five aspirants to be the new headmaster. The meeting may have been informal but it had serious intent: to take a view on which of the five would best meet the needs of the School. Malcolm Ward, the chairman, and the governors had reached the final stage in the selection process. Ward, John Whitehouse, the vice-chairman of governors, and Patrick Hutton, the retiring headmaster, had scrutinised all the applications; the five constituted the shortlist, none of them headmasters. Ward had chaired an interview panel which included Angus McIntyre, a senior don at Magdelen College, Oxford and chairman of the governors at Magdalen College School. He then took soundings among the staff. Florence Darby, the music teacher, remembered telling Ward that he had to appoint Bernard Trafford. The staff evidently found that the other four candidates were not to their liking. At any rate, the governors offered the post to Trafford.

In many respects he was the surprise choice. Ward, many years later, listed three factors which, in terms of orthodox appointments, Trafford had running against him. First, he was young, at 34 the third-youngest headmaster to be appointed at the School since Warren Derry; second, his academic subject

Portrait of Bernard Trafford, Headmaster 1990–2008.

Opposite page: Big Band members with Andy Proverbs and Roy Wood, 1998 (part of Sharing the Vision fundraising).

was music, so his route to a headmastership was unusual; third, his appointment was internal and the School had not made such an appointment since Henry Williams, exactly one hundred years before. What he had running for him was boundless enthusiasm, determination, ambition and a whole series of ideas about the School's development which, though inchoate at the time, had the possibility of forging an inclusive institution of different style from the past. He was late-20th century man, compared with his predecessor, whose beliefs and policies had more of a mid-century quality.

Like Hutton, he took over at a time of recession. Wolverhampton had hardly started to recover from the traumas of the industrial shakeout of the early 1980s, when the national economy turned down; the regional economy inevitably tightened up, starting in 1989. This happened as services had begun to take over from industry as the mainspring of the Midlands economy but, even so, as Trafford himself observed, 'every time Rover (the vehicles group) went into spasm, more small and medium-sized businesses went to the wall'. Local historian Chris Upton noted how, by the end of the 1980s, Wolverhampton Council had emerged as the biggest local employer. Wolverhampton's history had three constants, he suggested: growth, decay, change. When Trafford took up his new post, it looked as if Wolverhampton had moved into change, but it was stuttering change.

WOLVERHAMPTON GRAMMAR SCHOOL FOUNDED 1512

Bernard Trafford with pupils.

So there were outside pressures with which he had immediately to contend. The School, after a decade of independence, appeared strong. Yet every time the economy ran into difficulties, the number of families who could afford to send their children to a fee-paying school reduced. The School had to swim in a diminishing pool. This factor merged with another, as Trafford wrote:

The government of the day was already promoting competition between schools as a means of encouraging them to sharpen their performance, a tactic which became very much a feature of the early 1990s. The School was conscious of the need to work hard to recruit its fair share of students, not least because its academic selectivity, single-sex status and its need to charge fees immediately excluded many who might otherwise have liked to attend the School.

He felt that the School was simply not working as well as it might. Of course, he came into his post on the back of nine years' experience under Hutton, first as the head of music and then as head of the sixth form, so he was well attuned to the rhythms of the School. He believed, as he recollected

the circumstances of 1990, that the momentum achieved by Hutton in his earlier days had dissipated and that 'there was a slight feeling of not knowing where the School was going'. In his writing during later years, he observed that the A level results obtained by the School were not as good as they should or could be. He had told the selection panel of the need 'to bring the views of the staff on board'. What he wanted, he explained, was to unlock the talents in the staff room and along with that to make the School more student-centred, as he put it.

From the start, Trafford backed away from the traditional role of the headmaster in an institution like Wolverhampton Grammar School. His predecessors had been distant from the staff and remote from the boys, even if they had been friendly with the parents. There had been no habit of regular consultation with either staff or boys. He wanted an institution 'which enshrined the rights of students and teachers to a voice and promoted the expectation that they would participate'. He called it democracy. His drive to secure that, combined with the changes which took place in the shape of the School – its people and its buildings – led Ward to call the Trafford years 'exciting': 'there were things he thought needed to be changed; he found out what he wanted and carried everyone with him'.

Trafford's first move came on 28 August 1990 when he sent to the staff a closely typed memorandum of more than seven pages plus appendices and asked them to bring it with them to his first staff meeting on 3 September. Part of this memorandum dealt with minor matters of adjustment like changing the time of morning assembly and when letters should be sent to parents. But the change in style was quickly evident with a move to bring School behaviour more in line with the world outside:

> I think the time has come when we should move beyond the rather dated habit of referring to people by their surname: after we generally accord sixth formers the dignity of calling them by their Christian names when we get to know them a bit, and I would like to institute the practice of referring to pupils by their Christian names and, when we are calling out lists, where reasonable to use Christian name and surname.

The staff accepted this unanimously and Trafford looked back on that as the first collective decision of his headmastership. He wanted staff to become more involved in the School's public relations, to get away from "head-down" beavering away in isolation', to consider curriculum changes in light of the government-imposed national curriculum, to discuss homework, how to push pupils into taking more responsibility, pastoral care, discipline, staff career development (the polite term for 'appraisal'), methods of marking. There is, Trafford told the staff, an enormous amount of talking to be done and he took the first steps to fashion a committee structure which could undertake it. The School's academic committee would meet more often and he proposed to turn it into a think tank; heads of department should meet more regularly. There would be a weekly staff meeting, brief for the exchange of information, and a daily briefing of five minutes only on current matters by David Lambourne, the deputy headmaster.

Here, then, was what Trafford called his 'firm commitment to involving all the staff … in the process of making decisions about where this School is going'. One early step in this direction was to bring Lambourne back to the centre of affairs after he was sidelined by Hutton. 'Trafford was aware of the problem with Hutton. He didn't throw his weight around and he was only too happy to make me involved', Lambourne

recalled. The relationship between the new headmaster and his deputy could have been fragile, given that Trafford had been promoted above Lambourne. In fact, they created a durable partnership and Trafford remained grateful for his deputy's support.

But 'involving all the staff' was a complicated process, especially as neither Trafford nor the staff had any clearly elaborated plan as to how this might be achieved. The School, indeed, embarked on a running experiment, because it was not only the staff who became involved but also the boys and parents, through a process of consultation by questionnaire and direct contact. The notion of democracy meant that Trafford, of course, would allow his authority to be at least partially dispersed but, given the nature of his obligation to the governors, still have to accept the ultimate responsibility for the use of that authority. That would not necessarily be a problem if consultation could result in consensus, but arriving at that point put a premium on flows of information. Even 20 years later, members of staff of that time complained, justifiably or not, that a great deal of information was not passed on.

Certainly there were tussles of opinion and hence tussles of authority. Trafford later confessed that he found meetings with heads of department the most difficult. Arguments took place about who should be the chairman. More substantively,

WGS opens its doors to visitors.

This special issue of The Wulfrunian commemorated 130 years of the magazine.

the question of who should make policy quickly arose: if the heads of department, then Trafford gave over power granted to him by the governors; if the headmaster himself, then the heads of department became disenfranchised in terms of the democratic principles Trafford wished to follow. Resolution did not come until October 1995 when a minute of a meeting recorded:

Decision-making … HM welcomed participation in decision-making and insisted that HODs meeting could reach decisions where appropriate. This was happily accepted.

Another tussle involved a clash between headmaster and staff over whether boys should be present at the meetings when staff came together with parents. Parents wanted that but the staff did not and felt that they were being steamrollered into accepting it by the headmaster. Staff accused the head of trying to overturn one of their decisions. Trafford wrote in his diary the reaction of one teacher who said 'it was a funny sort of democracy when a No vote just means I come back later and try and reverse it'. In fact, the issue resolved itself after a trial period of meetings with boys present; the boys remained if the parents wanted them present.

Trafford moved to establish his think tank in spring 1992, when he thought that the School needed a new source to generate ideas and that teachers should have another means of making their voices heard. His original plan was to have a gathering of six teachers, but attendance usually was around ten. This group rapidly concluded that the School needed to define more closely what it was trying to achieve. Minutes of think tank meetings went on staff noticeboards with an invitation to make comments. From all of that came *The Challenge of Scholarship, The Spirit of Commitment*, the title of the Wolverhampton Grammar School philosophy. The School now had what, in corporate terms, was called a mission statement. Like companies, then following the fashion of 're-

engineering', the School had stripped down its work and set out the principles to make its work better:

The philosophy of Wolverhampton Grammar School places scholarship at the heart of a challenging education which promotes achievement through active involvement. It seeks to develop self-awareness and a sense of responsibility, values both individuality and altruism, and fosters the spirit of community and commitment traditional to the School.

From the early days of Trafford's headmastership, the staff had tried to set a course which rejected spoon-fed learning and, in effect, looked to a new relationship between teacher and student. It was not clear exactly how this might be brought about but Trafford was anxious, as he wrote later, that staff should concentrate on the question:

A staff meeting in my second term came to the conclusion without my prompting that we must give priority to developing ways of reducing students' dependency as learners and encouraging them to take real responsibility for their learning. That appeared, even at the time, an historic agreement.

This was the academic side of making the School, as Trafford termed it, more student-centred. Another facet of a School more student-centred was to give students more power to organise their community: a move towards the democracy Trafford was keen to inculcate. The most obvious manifestation of giving students greater power was a student council, the first elections for which took place in 1991. Student councils had a patchy history at Wolverhampton. When headmaster in the 1970s, Tony Stocks had started one, but this had been stopped by Hutton, his successor. Richard Williams, a student of the 1990s generation, celebrated re-birth in *The Wulfrunian*:

If 1992 has been notable for one thing, it must be that at last we, the pupils, are being given the chance to get together, air our views, and to force the issue by sheer numbers. This must be a good sign, for at last the staff's stranglehold over decision-making has gone. We, who are the majority, at last have at least a minor say in what goes on.

The council bedded in. Over the years it went through reorganisations – changes in the form of representation and so on, but it did not fade away through inertia. Trafford attached great significance to its very existence and contended in the November 2000 edition of the magazine, *Headlines*: 'there is no doubt that alienation and disaffection had been reduced and that there is an enormously increased sense of ownership and shared endeavour among students'. At the same time, he enjoyed the meetings:

> *Those Friday meetings of the student council are about the most stimulating of the week, really one of the best bits of the job. I am asked to explain why something is done – or why I can't change it. Frequently we plan together a significant improvement that will benefit everyone. I think it is important that the head is not only accessible but also accountable at those meetings.*

The *Headlines* article came under the banner, 'Much More Than Soggy Chips'. Business of the council, though, seems often to have been severely practical. In the first meeting, on 1 December 2000, after the publication of the *Headlines* article, the matters raised were tracksuits for sports teams; ketchup dispensers as against sachets at dinner; rules on hair colour; paying for lunch; bell in the library; demand for a girls basketball team; destination of money from confiscations; library opening hours; muddy paths; fence around the netball courts; student toilet time in lessons; confiscation of bags on top of lockers; and tickets for school buses.

Becky Griffiths, a year 13 student and chair of the council in 2002, contributing to an article in *Education Review*, saw great value in open discussion, the airing of complaints and methods of remedy:

> *Some students have extremely valid ideas that governors or teachers would never have thought of: pooling initiative results in extremely valuable changes. There are many examples of this having occurred in our own student council. Students have created various clubs and organisations initiated by a suggestion in the council.*

In one case the (also elected) senior prefects felt their responsibilities could be extended, which resulted in taking on some patrolling duties, thus broadening these prefects' influence and sense of responsibility.

First girls to start at the School aged 11 leaving in 1999.

By the time Becky Griffiths wrote about the student council's contribution to the running of the more democratic school, Trafford's ideas had become well entrenched and had wrenched the School away from the authoritarian style of school government. These changes in the School's culture had been taking place against a series of major developments which lined up the School for the 21st century.

New headmasters tend to be dissatisfied with the physical surroundings they inherit. Hutton quickly embarked on a building programme after independence. Trafford did the same, noting in *The Wulfrunian* that 'our accommodation

The new sports hall was opened in 1993.

from the staff when they were consulted. Trafford received just one letter from an angry parent and there was one Old Wulfrunian who sent his cap back. In social, though not in financial, terms, the governors had been tardy in making the move: Westminster School had started taking girls into its sixth form in 1977, and by 1984 all of the men's colleges at Oxford University had admitted women.

Still, it took a little time for the School to draw in girls. There were 17 out of a total of 90 first-year entrants in 1992, but the numbers in succeeding years climbed to 30 per cent and settled around 40 per cent in the second half of the 2000s. At first, the School could be relaxed about the number of entries. When the governors had started deliberating on the future development of the School, they had to bear in mind that if Labour won the 1992 general election, the assisted places scheme would disappear. This would reduce the size of the School's catchment area for new pupils. Co-education could offer some protection against that and, in any case, it would of itself widen the pool of potential entrants. As it happened Labour failed to win that election, so the governors had greater security of income, at least for a few years.

The key governor in pushing for expansion was John Whitehouse, an accountant who drew up a business plan. He could start in the knowledge that the funds drawn from the appeal of 1978–9 had been carefully husbanded and there was, according to Trafford, around £2m in the bank. The funds provided by the state for assisted places constituted a core of income. His plan demonstrated that the School could borrow money and finance its costs from the expanding revenue drawn from a larger population of students. In other words, new buildings and more students went together hand in hand.

So, reported Trafford in 1991, the School felt secure enough to take very bold steps:

Our £1.8m building programme, comprising extra new laboratories, classrooms and a truly magnificent sports hall with changing accommodation, will provide the extra facilities of which we have been feeling the lack for some years.

The first moves for a new sports hall had been taken in 1989 when John Johnson, the head of physical education, put his wish list of facilities on paper. This set off a chase around

has been barely adequate to provide the broad and varied curriculum that we offer'. In fact, the governors could adopt no other course if they pursued the policy of expansion which had swiftly been put in train during 1991.

The catalyst was the decision to make the School fully co-educational starting in September 1992. This decision had a degree of inevitability about it, given the presence of girls in the sixth form since 1984. The matter came up at the first governors' meeting Trafford attended in his new role: they set up a working party which could not find anybody against it; the opposite in fact – there was a wave of support, not least

comparable centres within 50 miles to check ideas and obtain advice. In 1993, Sir Jack Hayward, businessman and sometime owner of Wolverhampton Wanderers football club, formally opened the hall; this was a delicious and amiable revenge for him as the School had rejected his application for admission half a century before. 'The School's 650 pupils make superb use of the hall', reported the Wolverhampton *Express & Star*, with 'nine hours of sports hall action involving 250 of them every day'.

The following year work started on a new sixth form centre, at a cost of £1.75m, backing on to the 1981 library; there would be new teaching rooms, social areas and departmental offices. Probably, wrote Trafford in *The Wulfrunian*, the centre was the most ambitious building erected at the School since the main building was completed in 1875. It was the symbol of a new phase of expansion. On 1 March 1994, Dorothy Lepkowska reported in the *Birmingham Post* that the School had plans to increase the roll from 650 to 900 in three years and that five new teaching jobs would be created at the start of the next school year. She quoted Ward as saying that the School would have the most up-to-date facilities in the Midlands.

Much of the planning for this expansion fell on Lambourne, his calculations and projections, his planning

Opening of the sixth form centre, 1994.

Old Wulfrunian, Mervyn King, visiting the School in 2005.

Exam results day.

had been predicated on a roll of 840. The banking covenants had been tied to income and numbers of students. The School at no stage defaulted on its loans, but LloydsTSB, the School's bankers, seeing a falling roll, wanted their person on the board. The governors faced that off but still had to reduce the annual salary bill by £200,000. Salaries accounted for 75 per cent of the School's expenditure.

Trafford now started what he later called the most stressful phase of his career. Others might have said the same, because he felt obliged to make five redundancies. Rather than spreading uncertainty by taking one step at a time, he made the redundancies all at once. Nor did he adopt a last-in-first-out policy. 'My best friend on the staff was one of those who was made redundant', said Lambourne. This was Jim Chugg, the director of studies, the only holder of a senior post to depart. The other members of staff were off the academic mainstream, in the sports and music sections of the School. Anger quickly spread among the staff, centred on the unfortunate Angie Osborne, the business director. Informal meetings took place. For the first time since the 1930s, a feeling of insecurity came over the common room, although tempers calmed during the summer holidays. Lambourne recollected that 'sensible staff saw it was inevitable. Those chosen for redundancy were, on the whole, if it had to be someone – they were dispensable. Wiser counsels prevailed'.

The governors now had to deal with the problem of the loss of income and a falling roll. This would be gradual as those on assisted places would continue to take the benefits until the end of their school careers. The last money would come in 2004. But the government's move left the School weakened and challenged. Trafford calculated that the School needed to recruit two fee-paying pupils for every three pupils who had

for staffing and accommodation, as he projected forward from the School's existing position. 'The staff saw benefits in the building programme which provided security for their own jobs,' he recalled. But there were staff who, concerned about the future of assisted places, saw the expansion as over-ambitious, a dangerous option. Some look back and see the expansion after 1994 as being a strategic mistake. In retrospect it looked like that, but, in the mid-1990s, Ward, the governors and Trafford drew comfort from the terms of the assisted places legislation which required three years notice of closure. They had no thought of scaling down.

The position of the Conservative government weakened as the 1990s went on, so the arrival of the Labour government in 1997 did not surprise. What did surprise the School was the summary abandonment of assisted places. The government overrode the notice period and, suddenly, the School which had looked so strong confronted the painful consequences of retrenchment. Numbers had climbed to 797 and the staffing

A Hard Day's Midsummer Night's Dream, *2005.*

been on assisted places. The School thus resorted to an appeal, the third in 20 years. Called 'Sharing the Vision', it followed its predecessors in stressing the intent of providing bursaries for the less well-off. By the millennium, the appeal had raised about £1m. Students covered by bursaries of various types accounted for about eight per cent of the roll – ideally the

School would have liked 25 per cent. In 2003, the School spent £307,462 helping 62 students.

Ward saw through the problems of the late 1990s alongside Trafford, but retired as chairman of governors in 2001 to be succeeded by Simon Walford. Building stopped as expansive ideas dissipated. The 2000s were an altogether quieter decade

OpAL and Big Six.

than the 1990s. The School roll settled at around 670 and stayed that way into the 21st century. Confidence had returned by the middle of the 2000s and the last piece in Trafford's construction legacy was a new Arts Centre, with exhibition space and a drama studio, opened in November 2007.

Trafford's years as headmaster saw not only a sustained performance by the pupils in passing examinations, but also educational innovations and social experiences for the students of growing enrichment. Every year, pupils seemed to achieve higher results. In 2003, for example, there was a 98.5 per cent overall pass rate at A level and 72.9 per cent had been at

A or B grades. Consistently 80–85 per cent of the School's A level candidates went into their university of first choice. Such consistency impressed potential parents to the extent that the School attracted applications from pupils at other schools to join the sixth form. It also impressed the team from the independent schools inspectorate which, in 2001, found 'a very good school in all key areas', 'high quality of teaching' and a 'pastoral system well-managed'.

The effects of Trafford's early drive to raise participation and standards by this time had become effective, in that the inspectorate observed a policy of self-improvement and a system of monitoring it; academic departments had to report each year on their planned initiatives and how their plan for the previous year had fared. The think tank had emerged as an educational futures group to make recommendations on how the School should advance.

The ethos of the School demanded that it should find ways of enlarging the educational experience and widening its availability. Trafford was well aware, especially after 1997, that

Programme for the performance of Carmina Burana, 2008.

the more this could be done, the greater the attraction of the School and the greater the opportunities for raising revenue. Need could equal income. Two areas where this has taken place are in schemes called OpAL and Big Six.

OpAL, the acronym for Opportunities Through Assisted Learning, started from the desire of Ian Tyler, appointed in 1994 to teach English and drama and more recently the director of learning, to give his dyslexic sons a fulfilling academic life. He understood that a child with a phonological problem has a specific learning difficulty which is not related to intelligence. What the child therefore requires is specialised teaching to correct the difficulty. OpAL is designed to provide that; its name is chosen so that it looks like a subject and carries no overtones of remedial activity, perhaps making it socially difficult for the child. The teaching is intense – one teacher to two students – for 3.5 hours a week, as part of the normal academic regime. Over time the phonological weakness can be rectified. The number of OpAL students varies from 55 to 60, so around eight per cent of the School roll. Results came quickly: the first five OpAL students who took GCSE all obtained grades between C and A*, and half of those grades were A and A*. The governors saw merit in Tyler's advocacy of OpAL, not least because it could be self-

funding as parents would pay a premium for the service which could amount to a total of £500,000 a year.

Big Six emerged to meet the perceived shortcomings of the last year in primary schools when pupils prepare for their

Runners taking part in the annual Chris Walker Memorial Mile race.

Standard Assessment Tests (SATS). This is deemed a narrow and dismal experience. The School's idea was to replace that with a varied curriculum based on the concept of learning to learn. It was not to expand the sixth year of schooling with an early look at the seventh. This proved to be as much a new quest for the teachers as it was for the new pupils. As Trafford explained:

> *Teachers who normally expect to be in control of the*
> *learning had to learn to allow children to set the*
> *direction and help them follow it – wherever it went. The*
> *two English teachers involved, predictably maybe, took*
> *to the new approach with ease. For mathematicians and*
> *scientists it was arguably more challenging at first.*

The first year of Big Six drew 24 pupils and by the time of Trafford's final year as headmaster, the number had reached 40. For parents there is the relief that their children will not have to sit SATS and they have automatic entry to the senior school

WOLVERHAMPTON · GRAMMAR · SCHOOL
COAST TO COAST RUN FOR MUSCULAR DYSTROPHY

CUMBRIA
2,000ft.

YORKSHIRE

ST BEES HEAD

ROBIN HOODS BAY

SPIDEY·DEVILLE·WAGGY·OSC·RAJ BIR·SOPH·TUTTON·RHI·LIV&EM

26 – 27 · MAY · 2007.

The Annual Coast to Coast Run.

without examinations. For the School there is the benefit of a new revenue stream, as the fees are set at about 25 per cent less than for the senior school.

Of course, Trafford was well aware that at a time of rising educational results, the fact that the School held its own academically could not be enough to sustain its position and keep flowing a stream of new entrants. Hutton had realised that too. Both men had thus attached great importance to what the School did outside the classroom. As Trafford put it in a speech during 2002:

I believe passionately that the measurable things, such as exam results, are improved by the non-measurable, all those other things that make a real education … Government pressure to concentrate only on its utilitarian view of schooling is enormous … Government wants it both ways. It pushes and pushes schools to achieve higher

and higher exam scores, but when those scores rise there's a panic that standards are slipping.

Trafford was not afraid to see a school party depart for South Africa in the weeks before its members took GCSE exams: evidently they returned and took the papers with aplomb. As a musician he encouraged his own subject. In one year, taken at random, 2000, the School produced *Carmina Burana*, Carl

Trips, clockwise from the top: Picos 2006; skiing in Austria; Tanzania, 2005.

Annual Jazz Spectacular in Big School, 2004.

Overleaf: Preparing for Sports Day.

Orff's fusion of music, drama and dance; it started girls cricket; it had two endurance runs, coast-to-coast to raise money for charity; it sent the choir to Prague. All of that would have been in addition to the usual diet of school trips, sports events and society meetings.

In all of this, Trafford tried to set an example of participation, an example which extended his popularity and which took him into actions of which predecessors would never have dreamt. He would have a go at anything, Johnson said, and even trained himself to run long distance so he could take part in 'Xmasjogathon' with bacon butties afterwards. He abseiled down the tower of the School's main building for charity. Such activities showed Trafford seeking to push the School out into the community. For this, he had considerable flair. It showed at a number of different levels.

Trafford was a natural publicist, the ideal school advocate and public diplomat. He remained ready to talk with journalists: he had a ready talent for the quotable comment backed by strongly held views on the merits of independent education. In a different way he pushed the reputation of the School out into educational circles. Patrick Hutton, his predecessor, had taken the School into the Headmasters Conference (HMC), the representative body of British independent schools. Trafford took membership seriously, to the point of being elected chairman for 2007–8 and then asked to extend his term by a further year. He sought also to convey to both specialist and general public the impression of the School as innovative, pushing education out beyond the confines of the examination hall. This in turn led to the enhancement of his own reputation as an educational theorist, writing a doctoral thesis on democratic participation in schools and a steady stream of articles and books on the running of schools. Here he followed his own injunctions. He made demands on his staff to explore fresh methods of pedagogy: he engaged in his own quest.

Florence Darby contended that Trafford always did what he asked others to do, and when he decided to do something, he would see it through. And that applied to his departure. Invited to apply for the headmastership at Royal Grammar School, Newcastle, a bigger institution than Wolverhampton, he accepted out of curiosity and then decided to see it through. When the closing ceremonies on his Wolverhampton career took place in July 2008, tears were shed, and some belonged to him.

Mrs Felicity Hutton, Bernard Trafford and Charles Viner at the opening of the Arts Centre.

7 | TOWARDS THE 500TH ANNIVERSARY

Vincent Darby arrived at the School to succeed Bernard Trafford in September 2008. He came from the state system. At first sight this looked an unusual move: the School's governors might have been expected to appoint somebody from the independent sector in which Wolverhampton had been comfortably established for 30 years. Second sight showed there was nothing strange.

Darby's career had been spent in schools of the King Edward the Sixth Foundation, Birmingham, a body with an independent caste of thought which managed, it is true, two private schools but also five schools, voluntary aided with public funds, as, indeed, Wolverhampton had been during the post-war years. One of these was King Edward VI Camphill

School for Boys; there Darby had been headmaster, presiding over an institution which, governance apart, had much in common with Wolverhampton. In Camphill's own words, it offered 'academic excellence' and a 'breathtaking programme of extracurricular activities'. In other words, Camphill and Wolverhampton had the same ethos: they both wanted to provide a rounded and happy education.

Thus the switch for Darby was smooth at the educational level. But it was rather less easy in terms of the operational environment. Like Trafford, Patrick Hutton and Tony Stocks before him, Darby arrived at a difficult time for the city of Wolverhampton. Each assumed his post during an economic downturn. For more than 20 years, the local economy has been adapting to the loss of the dominating traditional industries in the metalworking and vehicle sectors by a switch into service sectors. Indeed, by 2008, as the City Council demonstrated, manufacturing's portion of business activity had shrunk to 11 per cent of companies engaged in Wolverhampton. Yet the diversification looked fragile: long-term unemployment remained high, the majority of job vacancies were in lower skilled occupations and there were five times as many applicants as posts available. The decline in manufacturing slowed during the first years of the 21st century, while banking, insurance and finance expanded. But even as Darby started at the School, the financial world tumbled into turmoil and an international recession began; Wolverhampton could not stand apart.

Trafford, looking back over his tenure, noted that it was always hard to fill the School, and most of his years coincided with economic expansion. Recessions made it harder still, as Hutton's anxiety showed during the first years of independence.

Clockwise from the top: Sports Day, 2010; Tennis on the Astroturf, 2010; Rugby 1st XV, 2007.

Given the competition from other schools, where no fees are demanded, Darby faced the immediate challenge of a slightly slipping roll, critical for an institution with finances in delicate equilibrium. As a registered charity, the School could not seek to make profits, but nor could it cope with regular loss. Like any business – and the School's turnover was about £6m – it tended to rely on borrowed funds for capital expansion and to use regular income to service and repay the loans. For that to work smoothly, the student roll had to hold steady at around 650–670.

Generally, recessions have a delayed impact on independent schools as most parents reduce educational spending only as a last resort. By the start of the 2009–10 academic year, Darby's second year, the School's roll stood at 648 pupils, of whom 393 were boys and 255 were girls, and, Darby noted, entries to Years Six and Seven had picked up as the School began to stem the fall in numbers. In testimony to the School's reputation, pupils came from other schools to study in the sixth form, making up about 10 per cent of the senior total. Recession had not dented the School's strength as an institution serving Wolverhampton and adjacent counties.

The strength, previous chapters have shown, evolved gradually. Darby found a school in good heart, as he put it. It remained so as it moved towards the 500th anniversary of its foundation, confident not only in its academic achievement but also in its ability to mount a range of activities outside the classroom. 'The School is developing the whole person', Darby asserted. 'Over the seven years of a school career, the pupil does exams but other things too.' Indeed, it is made clear in the 2009 handbook provided for all members of the School that these 'other things' have great importance:

> WGS strongly encourages all students to participate fully and actively in the breadth of school life whether through sport, music, drama, outdoor pursuits, debating, or through a wealth of other clubs and societies. Equally, we encourage students to be involved, at an appropriate level, in helping run the school through such vehicles as Student Parliament and Peer Support.

For Darby, the exam results announced in summer 2009 capped a remarkable first year. More than that, they extended the run of habitual success. For the third year running, Advanced Level students had a 100 per cent pass rate with 77 per cent of the results recorded at A and B grades. For the eighth year running, all of the Advanced Level art students received A grades. At a practical level, this meant that the majority of pupils gained admission to the universities of first choice. The effect was to enhance the School's reputation as an institution providing a secure grounding for its pupils, thus feeding into the effort to hold steady the numbers on the student roll.

The reputation springs from consistency: generations of staff, from the days of Thomas Beach, have drawn high levels of performance from the pupils. Statistical analysis by the Centre for Evaluation and Monitoring at Durham University has shown how the teaching and learning processes adopted by the 21st-century generation of staff, in terms of adding value to the basic study of the syllabus, have taken the School into the higher reaches of independent schools. Exam results have placed the School in the top half of these institutions.

The teaching framework has been based on what might be classified as 'national curriculum plus'. 'The framework allows us to use the national curriculum but not be hidebound by it.

Big Sixers enjoying lunch in the Derry Hall, 2010.

Pupils can develop interests. They are not bound by standard assessment tests [SATS]', observed Darby. Once pupils have started the approach to GCSE, the teaching naturally has been more attuned to the normal requirements of the exams. In part, this teaching policy is related to the School's competitive position. Like Trafford before him, Darby has recognised that 'state schools are better, they have improved markedly; independent schools have to ensure a marked difference'.

The concomitant of the scholarly work at the School has been traditionally what Darby called 'other things', the range of activities set out in the 2009 handbook, the encouragement to participate. In independent schools, onwards from the influence of Rugby's Thomas Arnold in the mid-19th century, the favoured extracurricular activity has been sport. Wolverhampton has followed that line to some degree, notable in the 21st century for the variety of its offering: more than a dozen activities, the School reported to the Charity Commissioners, from rounders to shooting, from football to netball, from cricket to squash. For the most part internal competition, fostered in the 20th century, has been replaced by contests with other schools; although relatively small, 'the School has managed to punch above its weight – in football, for example, we hold our own against bigger schools', Darby commented.

For Darby, sport is only part of the educational package which, unwrapped, is designed to develop the whole person. 'I have pride in seeing youngsters getting involved in everything:

Music plays a central role in the life of the School.

Performers at the Jazz Spectacular, 2008.

footballers and netballers playing on Saturday, rehearsing for a play or music performance on Monday and Tuesday. Our music is strong and I regard it as every bit as important as sport.'

Indeed, the School has shone as a beacon of the arts, made brighter by the 2008 completion of, first, the Viner Arts Centre, named after a veteran art teacher who a year after his own centenary staged in the eponymous space his own exhibition, and, second, the Hutton Theatre, named after the School's first headmaster after independence.

Andrew Clark, writing in the *Financial Times* of 18 April 2009, observed how 'the idea that music helps to create rounded human beings has long been lost on policymakers in the west, with the result that music education is now heavily dependent on local initiative'. In the Wolverhampton area, the School is an example of that initiative, with a history stretching back over a hundred years of performances of all types, often in aid of charities like the nearby Compton Hospice. In 2008–9, the School had different choirs for different age groups, amalgamating to take part, for example, in a regional production with the City of Birmingham Symphony Orchestra and its own production of Carl Orff's *Carmina Burana*. It had its own orchestra and smaller groups like a string orchestra plus different bands for jazz and concert work.

The Hutton Theatre immediately became the home for plays both on and off the syllabus. The inaugural production was Shakespeare's *As You Like It*, followed by Rudyard Kipling's *The Jungle Book*, which had a hundred students active onstage and backstage, and Robert Louis Stevenson's *Treasure Island*.

'We do plays and treat the actors as professionals; we don't do "school plays"', said Ian Tyler, the School's head of teaching and learning, a trained actor himself who came to the School originally to teach English and drama. For him, the productions are a means of imbuing students with something beyond the curriculum, of taking intellectual curiosity out of the classroom and fostering a spirit of inclusion: 'the value of the School is outside the curriculum'.

Inclusion has proved a vital factor in the development of the School; it is the binding which ensures the ability to adapt, and managing adaptation is always and inevitably at the back of Darby's mind:

> *The School has changed more in the last 40 years than in the previous 140. There was no fundamental change from 1870 to 1970. Now change continues at an exponential rate. The School has maintained a speed of change while maintaining its traditional ethos.*

In handling change, the School has the advantage of size: 'We have all the advantages of a small school: the strength of being a community, the relations between students and staff, the relations between staff and parents. Small is indeed beautiful'.

In the approach to its quincentenary, there have been three distinct phenomena to which the School has been obliged to

respond. First, it has ceased to be a local institution meeting local needs, sending boys out into the local economy. Rather, it has become a local institution meeting national professional and commercial needs, coping with the greater fluidity of a labour market, where a person might have several careers over one working life. The boys and girls of Wolverhampton see a broader future than the pupils of two generations ago.

Top: A level students in the new Viner complex.

Above: 'Who Cares?' Theatre studies production, 2009.

129

At the same time, and second, the population mix of Wolverhampton has leavened: the arrival in Wolverhampton of immigrants, largely from the Indian sub-continent, changed the town and eventually the make-up of the School roll. The 2001 census showed that Asians made up 14.3 per cent of Wolverhampton's population and that is roughly their proportion of School pupils.

Third, social and hierarchical barriers have eroded. The young no longer accepted so readily the diktat of the old. The Thatcher years especially glorified the individual. Educational expectations for girls have become as high as they have been historically for boys. Hence the collapse of gender discrimination in the older and traditional institutions like Oxford and Cambridge colleges and, indeed, Wolverhampton Grammar School.

Carried into the School, this combination of phenomena had distinct effects. 'Teachers are better to the boys when the girls are there', suggested Nic Anderson, who started at the School as a pupil, returned as a teacher and became deputy head in 2009, and thus able to chart the difference. The masculine atmosphere of the School softened, other teachers agreed; students became better mannered once girls became part of the social mix.

This chimed with a change in techniques as teachers came to terms with the more relaxed ambience and a shifting relationship with pupils. In his schooldays, Anderson recalled,

Big Sixers, 2009.

habitually there was 'blackboard teaching with a textbook of some description; it was a one-way relationship where the teacher delivered and the student accepted'. In the 21st century, he explained, 'the teacher is part of the classroom, the student can answer back'. In any case, just as students are subject to continual assessment so are teachers answerable to a range of interested parties: the students themselves, the parents, their colleagues. The days have gone when the door shut behind the teacher as he or she entered the classroom and was left to proceed how he or she pleased. The School has adopted what Ian Tyler termed 'the idea of the teaching profession being inquisitive about its own practice'. Teachers are 'not just filling vessels', they are now 'bringing creativity to education'. In short, as Darby pointed out, the teachers are not isolated in the classroom, teaching has become more open, more accountable and, at the School, they are becoming more robust in the way they review their work.

In sum, Darby commented:

The School is more attuned to the needs of the students for the 21st century. There is always a place for scholarly work, but it is pitched at the needs of modern life. Schools have to be more professional in the way they deal with youngsters.

It follows from this that the School itself has become a more complex organisation. While Hutton and his predecessors delegated some responsibility to heads of the academic departments, Trafford and Darby after him have established representative groups which examine areas like curriculum development, assessment and reporting, careers, personal and social education, outdoor education and the gamut of extracurricular activities. These groups cut across the narrow academic disciplines and give a voice to all members of staff that can shape and influence policy. The staff have assumed responsibilities in a way which headmasters up to the 1990s would not have countenanced.

While methods have changed to keep pace with broader movements in society at large, there is nevertheless a continuity of approach at the School. This is evident in the School's local position. Hutton and Trafford before him would agree with Darby that:

Within the city we have the reputation of being the leading school in the area but we're not accessible to all. One of the key issues for the Grammar School is that it is still seen as Wulfrunian and we do as much as possible to be accessible and, in a broader context, to spread an educational vision in the city.

One way in which this might happen, and which Darby is keen to encourage, is for senior students to go into local primary schools to support struggling youngsters. This is a tiny example of the sort of altruism which led to the establishment of the School by Sir Stephen Jenyns.

The aura of Jenyns hovers over the School. It is partly present through the continuing association of Merchant Taylors' in the affairs of the School: the guild, from which Jenyns came, controlled the School at a distance during the early days and now can influence it through membership of the governing body. But more than that, Jenyns's aim of sponsoring a school for 'good manners and learning' holds good 500 years later, giving the institution the hard foundation of constant purpose. Of that, Vincent Darby is sure:

The School has changed so much in its first 500 years – achieving great things and building up a reputation for educational excellence. And yet, despite the School's expansion and development, the vision of 'learning and good manners' that Sir Stephen Jenyns had for his 'faire grammar school' in 1512 remains at the heart of our busy, happy and very successful school today. Indeed, his wise words will be the cornerstone of the continued growth and progress of WGS in the future – a future we look to, as Wolverhampton's Grammar School, with confidence, with ambition and with a real sense of adventure.

Walking between lessons, 2010.

Overleaf: Big Sixers start their WGS adventure, 2006.

I | THE HEADMASTERS

Pre 1550	William Devey
1569–73	* Raby
1573–1605	Thomas Maddox
1605–10	Richard Barnes
1610–27	William Wilson
1627–30	Jervas Needham
1630–58	Daniel Rawlett
1658–78	John Coles
1678–80	Samuel King
1680–5	Isaac Backhouse
1685–1710	John Plymley
1710–29	Robert Daubrie
1729–38	Robert Cartwright
1738–59	John Southwell
1760–8	Benjamin Clement
1768–83	William Robertson
1783–5	Vacant
1785–99	William Lawson
1799–1830	William Tindall
1831–55	William White
1855–63	Thomas Campbell
1863–4	Walter Wood
1865–89	Thomas Beach
1890–5	Henry Williams
1895–1905	James Hichens
1905–23	Watson Caldecott
1923–9	Walter Booth
1929–56	Warren Derry
1956–72	Ernest Taylor
1972–8	Anthony Stocks
1978–90	Patrick Hutton
1990–2008	Bernard Trafford
2008–	Vincent Darby

* No record of forename

Vincent Darby,
Head 2008.

II | HELPFUL BOOKS

Barnsby, GJ *Socialism in Birmingham and the Black Country, 1850–1939,* Wolverhampton, Integrated Publishing Services, 1998.

Court, WHB *The Rise of the Midland Industries, 1600–1838,* Oxford, Oxford University Press, 1938.

Griffith, G *Going to Markets and Grammar Schools,* London, William Freeman, 1870.

Jones, WH *Story of the Municipal Life of Wolverhampton,* London, Alexander and Shepheard, 1903.

Lapping, B *The Labour Government, 1964–70,* London, Penguin Books, 1970.

Linton, D *Wolverhampton Grammar School,* Stroud, Tempus Publishing, 2000.

Mander, GP *The History of the Wolverhampton Grammar School,* Wolverhampton, Old Grammar School Press, 1913.

Marwick, A *British Society since 1945,* 4th edition, London, Penguin Books, 2003.

Mason, F *The Book of Wolverhampton,* Buckingham, Barracuda Books, 1979.

Medlicott, WN *Contemporary England,* London, Longmans Green, 1967.

Philips, D *Riots and Public Order in the Black Country, 1835–1860* in Stevenson, J and Quinault, R (eds), *Popular Protest and Public Order,* London, George Allen & Unwin, 1974.

Taylor, AJP *English History, 1914–45,* Oxford, Oxford University Press, 1965.

Timmins, N *The Five Giants, a biography of the welfare state,* London, Fontana Press, 1996.

Upton, C *A History of Wolverhampton,* Chichester, Phillimore, 1998.

A Level Art, 2009.

Overleaf: Leavers, 2007.

Index

Locations for illustrations are shown in **bold.**

Abernethy, John 14, **26**
abseiling **70**, 121
accessability 132
accountability 131
accounts (subject) 29
aerial view **10–11**
Aggleton, PJ 84
air raid shelters 63
Air Training Corps **63**
A-Levels
    1963 77
    2009 127
    art **139**
    Hutton 108
    Trafford 116
allotments 63
Anderson, Nic 130
Apathy Society 71
Appleby, John 79
architect's drawing **38–9**
archive 9
Army Air Corps **103**
Arnold, Thomas 30, 40, 127
art 59, **139**
Arts Centre 116, **121**, 128
As You Like It (William Shakespeare) 128
Asians 130
assembly 71, **88**, 104, 109, **124**
assisted places scheme 98–9, 103, 114
association football – *see* football
Association of Friends of the School 100
Association of Voluntary Aided Schools 80
astroturf **126**
athletics 40, **61**
Austria **120**
Aviation Society **103**

Backhouse, Isaac 136
Balloon Fundraising Day **102**
Bank of England 14
Barnes, Richard 22, **23**, 136

Barnsby, GJ 41, 45
Barnshaw, Mrs M 65
BBC 14, 50
Beach, Thomas
    academic results 40
    appearance 33
    background 32
    cartoon of **32**
    character 41
    consistency from his time 127
    departure 41–2
    foundation laying 44
    legacy 12, 41
    listed 136
    photograph **36**
    pivotal role 33, 36
    sport 40
    Wulfrunian 38
Bennett 64
Benson, AET 14
Biarritz 61
Big Band **107**
Big Room 32
Big School
    assembly 71, **88, 124**
    Coat of Arms **152**
    concert **52–3**
    early 1920s 51
    extending space 76
    Founder's Day **58**
    gallery construction 104
    Jazz Spectacular **121**
    lessons **37**, 38
    Oxbridge honours board **15**
    plaque honouring Caldecott **45**
    stained glass **18, 20, 60, 65, 90**
    War Memorial **49, 65**
    weather vane **13**
    window replacement 59
Big Six 117–19
    2009 **131**
    an innovative programme 12
    lunch in Derry Hall **127**
    students at work **101, 105, 116, 133–5**

Bilston 20
biology
    Derry's lack of 69
    girls 102
    new laboratory 97, 98, 103
    Taylor introduces 74
Bird, John 88, 92
Birmingham Post 113
Black Country 40
Blackburn Rovers FC 82
Board of Education 42, 43
boarders
    accommodation 38, **70**
    decline in numbers 62
    earliest recorded 18
    priorities 30
    School House 44
book keeping 44
Booth, Walter 54, **54**, 56–7, 136
Bowen, H. 47
Boxing Club 47, 61, **66**
Boy Scouts 61, 62, 78, 83
Boyd, Robert James **64**
Brandon, Robert 74, 77–8, 86, 97
brass band **78, 95**, 98
British Empire 62
Brockless, Keith 87
Brocton Camp **48**
Bromsgrove 18
Brook, Norman 14, **48**, 50
Brookes, Stanley **48**
Brough, Connie
    appointed 82
    Hallmark's legacy 90
    on Hutton 97, 99
    school's removal from State system 88
buckles 25
building programmes
    Booth 57
    Hutton 104
    Merridale Building 59
    science 45, 71
    Stocks 86
    Trafford 111–14

The first of four embroidered panels produced to celebrate 500 years of WGS.

bursaries
    increasing numbers planned 15
    limited numbers 98
    'Sharing the Vision' appeal 115
    Stocks's appeal 90, 96
    various 115
Burton, William 21
Butler, RA 92

Caldecott, Watson
    eulogised 50
    examination results 49
    legacy 54, 56
    listed 136
    photographs **45, 49**
    portrait **51**
    resigns 51
    tenure 44–5
Cambridge University
    Beach 32
Caldecott's report 49
    early days of WGS 24
    football blues 100
    gender discrimination 130

Hichens, success rates under 44
    scholarships 62, 69, 74
Campbell, Revd Thomas 30–2, **31**
    Beach and 33, 40
    complains of school environment 28
    cricket 40
    listed 136
canings 29, 65–6 – *see also* corporal
    punishment; discipline
Cannock Chase 70, 79
capital development programme 14
capitation fees 20, 30–2, 42
caps 30, **54, 55**, 112
Carhart, William 70
Carmen Wulfrunense 47, **47**
Carmina Burana (Carl Orff) **117**, 119, 121,
    128
Cartwright, Robert 136
Castlecroft **65**
catechism 27, 44
Centre for Evaluation and Monitoring,
    Durham University 127
Chaddesley Corbett 18, **19**
*Challenge of Scholarship, The Spirit of
    Commitment, The* 110
Chancery Court 22, 24, 26, 30
change 129
changing rooms 45, 76
Channel Tunnel 40
Charity Commissioners
    abortive land purchase 1861 31
    curriculum changes 41
    delays approving move 1870s 33
    school's sports report 127
    Tindall's complaint to 28
Cheltenham College 42
chemistry 42, 44, 69, 99
chess 63–4, 78, **92**, 128
choir **69**, 78, 121
Cholmondeley, Allan 57
Choral Society 61
Chrees, William 26
Chris Walker Memorial Mile **118**
Christianity 30, 58 – *see also* Church of
    England
Chugg, Jim 114
Church of England
    clergyman headmasters 20, 32
    headmaster and ushers 30, 32
    influence wanes 27, 29
    Roman Catholic recusants and 22

City of Birmingham Symphony Orchestra
    128
Civil War 20, 22, 23
Clark, Andrew 128
classics
    1840 citizens' memorandum 29
    1901 44
    1957 74
    Caldecott 45
    Derry 69
    mathematics and 51, 69
    sixth form **68**
Clement, Benjamin 136
Clodd, Ernest 50, 51
coal 20–1, 25, 41
Coast, David 62, 63, 65
Coast to Coast Run **118–119**
coats of Arms **60, 152**
co-education 12, 100, 112 – *see also* girls
Coles, John 136
Collegiate Church 36
Combined Cadet Force 70, 79
Common Room (sixth form) **104**
comprehensive education
    circulars 86
    Crosland 82
    Hattersley 83
    Hutton on 96
    Parkfields 88
Compton Hospice 128
Compton Road
    carved masonry **33**
    frontage extended 46
    Headmaster's house 76
    move to 12, **21**, 41
    new buildings 43
    prospectus describes 38
    vacant houses acquired 104
computers **97, 104, 130**
concerts 46, **52–3**, 70, **95**, 98 – *see also*
    music
Conservative Party 95, 96, 114
Cooper, Robin 69
corporal punishment 29, 33, 65–6 – *see also*
    discipline
Court, WHB 20, 25
Court of Appeal 93
Court of Chancery 22, 24, 26, 30
Court of Queen's Bench 24
Craigmyles 90
crests **8**

cricket
    1890 **40**
    1928 **56**
    1937 62
    builds reputation for 40
    girls 121
    long-distance views **16–17, 59**
    Memorial Grounds **65**
Crickmay, Francis 50, 54
Crosland, Anthony 82
cross-country running 50
CSEs 84
curricula
    16th Century 20
    post Merchant Taylors' 27
    1840 citizens' memorandum 29
    1854 scheme of arrangement 31
    1901 44
    1960s 78
    Derry 69
    Hichens 43
    learning to learn 118
    science in 41, 42
    Stocks remodels 86

Dance, EH (Dickie) 44, 51
dance band 61
Darby, Abraham 21
Darby, Florence 78, 98, 106, 121
Darby, John
    appointed 69
    on co-education 100
    on Hutton 100
    on Taylor 74, 83
    wife 98
Darby, Vincent
    accessibility of school 132
    adaptation, importance of 129
    appointed 124
    background 124
    exam results 127
    Hutton and 131, 132
    introduction by 12–15
    listed 136
    numbers 126
    photographs **12, 137**
    representative groups 131
Dark Ages 20
Dartmouth, Earl of 45
Daubrie, Robert 136
dayboys 30, 44

Debating Society
    British Empire 62
    classical or modern education 47, 49
    founded 40
    World War I 47
    Wulfrunian 40, 61
Delville Wood 46
Derry, Warren 57–62
    anecdotes about 70
    Booth and 54
    canings 65
    crowning years 68–70
    depicted **58, 71**
    Derry Building 76
    Education Act 1944 66–7
    Founder's Days 58, **58**, 60, 62, 64, 69
    a giant 57
    importance of 12
    listed 136
    retires 71
    successor 74
Derry Building **76, 86**
Derry Hall 15, **127**
Devey, William 136
'Dig for Victory' **62**
dining hall 76, **76**
Diocesan Board of Education 29
direct grant schools
    abolition of 98
    becomes one 43
    ministry of education hesitates 68
    preference for 67
    Stocks on 87
discipline 29, 54, 70, 102 – *see also* canings;
    corporal punishment
drama
    Booth encourages 56
    fine reputation for 14
    Hutton Theatre 128–9
    Hutton's competitions 98
    post World War II resumption 70
    studio 116
drawing 27, 30, 44
Droitwich 18
Dudley, Dud 21
Dudley Castle Hill **22**
Dulwich College 54
Dunedin 32
Durham University 30, 127
dyslexia 117

East House 44
Edelman, Miss C 65
Edinburgh Academy 57
Education Act 1902 42
Education Act 1944 67, 70, 80, 92
Education Act 1976 88
Education Review 111
electricity and magnetism (subject) 44
Elementary Education Act 1870 41
Elizabeth II, Queen 74, **75–6**, 76
embroidered panels **144, 147–8, 151**
Encyclopedia Britannica 44
Endowed Schools Bill 33
English (subject) 29, 44, 56, **86**
English History (AJP Taylor) 59
English literature (subject) 44
Evesham 63
examinations
    1st three hundred years 23
    1885 40
    1898 Cambridge 44
    Caldecott 49
    Darby 127
    Derry 61
    eleven-plus 80, 83
    entrance 97
    results **114**
    Trafford 116
examiners 31
Express & Star 87, 88, 96, 113
extracurricular activity
    1930s 61
    Booth 56
    Camphill 124
    Darby 127
    Hutton 98, 100
    Taylor 78
    Trafford 119, 121
    Tyler 129

fees 92, 98, 119
Financial Times 128
firewatching 63
first aid club 56
Five Giants, The (Nicholas Timmins) 9
Flewker, Herbert 41
football
    Beach introduces 40
    1902–3 **46**
    1924–5 **56**
    1930s new system 61

1937 62
Oxbridge blues 100
21st Century 127
Founder's Day
  1903 43
  Caldecott's first 45
  1918 49
  Derry and 58, **58**, 60, 62, 64, 69
  1945 67
  1947 69
  1957 76
  1966 78
  1969 77
  1974 86
  St Peter's Church **34–5**
  2011 15
France 26
free hand drawing 44 – *see also* drawing
French (subject) 27, 30, 44
front lawn **69–70**
fundraising
  co-education 100
  Hichens 42
  Hutton 104
  Kettle 36
  'Sharing the Vision' 115
  Ward 90
Fuoss, Jakob 50

GCSEs 117, 127
General Certificate of Education (GCE) 70
geography 29, **86, 125**
geometrical drawing 44
Gerald Mander Room **7**
German (subject) 27, 30, 44
'GHT' 50
girls
  cricket 121
  educational expectation 130
  effect of 102
  first intake 100, **100**
  first intake at 11 **111**
  numbers rising 112
  proportion of in 2010 12
Glasgow 50
Goatfell Summit **79**
'Golden Slumbers' 69
Gooch, John 29
grammar (subject) 29
'Grammar Faces A Slow Death'
  (Wolverhampton *Express & Star*) 87

grammar schools
  19th Century 24
  comprehensives and 80, 87
  Education Act 1944 67
  Hutton on 96
  one of the best four 66
  Taylor on 77, 82
Grayson, Denis 86, 88
Great Depression 41, 42, 58
Great Hall – *see* Big School
Great Western Railway 41
Greek (subject) 44
Greeks 20
Griffith, G 24
Griffiths, Becky 111
Grow More Food (campaign) 63
Gulbenkian Award 80
gymnasium
  Hallmark building 77, **87**
  Old Wulfrunians gift 49, **50**
  wish list 43

Hallmark, Henry
  Hallmark building 77, **87**
  legacy 90
  mentioned on plaque **21**
  retires 83
  stained glass panel **90**
Hallmark building 77
Hallmark gym **87**
Hard Day's Midsummer Night's Dream, A **115**
Harding, JB **48**
Hardy Spicer propellor factory 67
Harrow School 14, 20
Hartree, Victor 83, 99
Hattersley, Roy 83
Hayward, Sir Jack 113
Headlines 111
Headmasters Conference (HMC) 121
Headmaster's study **104**
heat (subject) 44
Heidelberg 61
Henry VIII, King 18
Hewins, WAS 14
Hichens, James 42–4, **42**, 45, 51, 136
High Green, Queen Square **28**
history 29, 69, 77, 102
History of Wolverhampton, A (Chris Upton) 9
Holmes, Roy 62, 66, 83
Homer 21
Homer, John **58**, 60

Homer House 70
homework **29**, 78
Horace 21
Horrell, HBC 68
house system 44, 70
Howitt, AW **96**
humanities 15, 77 – *see also* individual
  subjects
Hutton, Felicity **121**
Hutton, Patrick 93–100
  appointed 93
  building programme 104
  Darby and 131, 132
  extra curricular activity 98, 100, 119
  full independence 12, 96–7, 124
  improvement of facilities 103
  Lambourne 109
  listed 136
  photographs **93, 94, 96, 102**
  retires 106
  specification 95
  student coucil 110
  Trafford on 108
  'weeding out' 99
Hutton Theatre 128

immigration 130
Importance of Being Earnest, The
  (Oscar Wilde) 56
inauguration 36
independence
  bedding in 103
  celebratory concert **95**
  choices 67, 82
  Hutton 96
  inspectorate 116
  older staff's feelings 93
  public reaction 97
  support for 76, 97
  Trafford on 121
  Wolverhampton Council and 87–8
  Wulfrunian on 98
Independence Appeal 96
Indian sub-continent 130
Industrial Revolution 20, 27
influenza 50
Inner London Education Authority 93
Inspection Report 2007 14
Ireland 40
iron 21, 41, 43
IT **97, 104, 130**

japanning 25–6, 27, 28
Jazz Spectacular **121, 128** – *see also* music
Jenyns, Sir Stephen
    aura remains 132
    basis of his fortune 12
    coal 20
    Founder's Day 43
    giving back 18
    plaque **21**
    Rushock estate 36
    stained glass window **20**, 59
Jenyns House 70
John Roper Room **103**
Johnson, John 93, 97, 112
Johnson, Lynne 9, **96**
Jones, William 28
Jungle Book, The (Rudyard Kipling) 128
junior school
    1911 **43**, 46, **46**
    Hichens reorganises 44
    1969 demolition 76–7, **77**
    2010 plans for 15

Kent, HRH Duchess of **103**
Kenyon, Lord 24
Kettle, Rupert
    chairman of trustees 33, 36, 60
    illness 42
    photograph **42**
Keynes, John Maynard 59
Kidderminster 18, 51
King, Mervyn 14, **114**
King, Samuel 136
King Edward the Sixth Foundation,
    Birmingham 124
King Edward VI Camphill School for Boys
    124
Kipling, Rudyard 128

Labour Party
    Great Depression 58
    local government 87, 88, 95–6;
    1964 election 80
    1974 election 83
    1992 election 112
Lambourne, David
    appointed 83
    daily briefing 109
    Oxbridge problem 86
    planning sixth form centre 113–14
    school status 87

sidelined 99
    on Trafford's redundancies 114
Langton, Colonel **96**
language laboratory **92** – *see also* modern
    languages
languages – *see* classics; French; German;
    Latin; modern languages
Lapping, Brian 80
Lapsley, John 14
Latin 20, 44, 57, 102 – *see also* classics
Lawson, William 136
'learning to learn' 118
Leek, BM 70
Lepkowska, Dorothy 113
Leveson family 22
libraries
    1st library (Hichens) 44, 45
    building programme 86
    bullying of librarians 102–3
    girls 102
    Merridale Building 59, **84**
    sixth form **85**
    Stephen Jenyns Library **96**, 97, 98, 113
Lichfield, Bishop of 20
Linton, Deirdre 9, 57, 102
Lion Hotel, Kidderminster 51
Lister laboratory **97**
Lloyds TSB 114
lockmakers 25, 45
London 21, 33, 51, 87
London School of Economics 14
Ludlow 83

Maddox, Thomas 136
Magdalen College, Oxford 106
Magdalen College School 106
Mander, Gerald
    acknowledged 9
    assessments of Merchant Taylors'
    problems 21, 22, 24
    Campbell's years 30
    death 71
    direct grant status, preference for 67
    Education Act 1944, build-up to 66
    Jenyns's stained glass windows 65
    late 19th century pressure to teach
    science 41
    Merchant Taylors' integrity 26
    new trustees 26–7
    pupil numbers 26
    Rawlett 22

    standard work on WGS 18
    upper and lower school 32
    White, William 28
    Williams, Henry 42
Mander, Philip 83, 93
Mander family 12, 57
Manders Property (Wolverhampton) Ltd **21**
map reading **105**
marble fireplace, Gerald Mander Room **7**
marine biology **78** – *see also* biology
Markham, Eric **64**
Marston, John 44, **44**, 45, 50
Marston family 12
Marston House 70
Martin, Alan 92
Marwick, Arthur 83
Mason, F 27, 28
Mason, Stanley 14
mathematics
    1840 citizens' memorandum 29
    1957 74
    Derry 69
    learning to learn 118
    own classroom 51

streaming 86
McIntyre, Angus 106
mechanics institutes 27
Medlicott, WN 80
Memorial Grounds **65**
Merchant Taylors'
   1875 inauguration 36
   breakdown of relations 12
   Chancery case 22, 24, 26
   coat of arms **60**
   conflicts of interest 21
   continuing association 132
   educational activities 20
   Hutton with **102**
   Jenyns as warden 18
   members who were original benefactors 18
   recusants, attitude to 22
   resigns as trustee 25, **25**
   Rushock estate 36
   St Peter's gallery 23, **23**
   Stephen Jenyns Library opening **96**
   trusteeship years 21, 23
Merridale Building **59, 68, 84**
Merridale Farm 33

Merridale Lane 51, 59
metalworkers 25, 27, 58, 124
Methuen, Lord **58**
Midland Counties Express 67
Midlands
   commercial and industrial sector 95
   Court's history of 20
   most up-to-date facilities in 113
   movements of labour 45
   services replace industry 106
Ministry of Education 67, 71, 76
mission statement 110
model drawing 44
modern languages 15, 56, 74 – *see also*
   French; German
Molineux family 26
Moore, RW 14, 20
Moreton, John 60
Moreton House 70
Morning Chronicle 32
motor industry
   20th Century, dawn of 45
   1920s and 30s 58
   1950s 74
   Rover 106
   21st Century 1 24
'Much More Than Soggy Chips' (*Headlines*)
   111
Municipal Grammar School 63
music
   Big Band **107**
   Big School concert **52–3**
   brass bands **78, 95**, 98
   choir **69**, 78, 121
   choral society 61
   concerts 46, **52–3**, 70, **95**, 98
   dance band 61
   Jazz Spectacular **121, 128**
   miscellaneous **128**
   music room 77
   orchestra 46
   organ 98
   'part of life' 94
   reputation for 14
   Rust's impetus 65
   a specialist music school? 87
Mytchett Camp **57**

N. Budd & Son **41**
national curriculum – *see* curricula
'national curriculum plus' 127 – *see also*

curricula
National schools 29
Natural History Society 47
Nechells, John 18, **18**, 60
Nechells House 70
Needham, Jervas 136
Newnham, CA 42
Nigeria 14
Normanbrook, Lord 14, **48**, 50
North House 44
Norton, Dennis 90

Officer Training Corps – *see* OTC
Offley, Thomas 18, **18**, 60
Offley House 70
Old Boys cricket team **56**
Old Library **84** – *see also* libraries
Old Wulfrunians
   Brook 50
   football blues 100
   girl pupils, attitude to 100
   independence issue 82
   Mander family 57
   World War II 66
Old Wulfrunians Association
   1967 dinner 82
   financial support 58
   geographical spread 90
   growth of 49
   gymnasium 49, **50**
   local source of support 58
   Mander 71
   Taylor addresses 80
   Taylor's appeal 76
O-Levels 84
OpAL (Opportunities Through Assisted
   Learning) 12, **116**, 117
open-air theatre 56, 63 – *see also* drama
orchestra 46 – *see also* music
Orff, Carl 119, 121, 128
organ 98 – *see also* music
Osborne, Angie 114
OTC
   annual camps 61
   Brocton Camp **48**
   establishment 48
   Mytchett Camp **57**
   record numbers 62
   security of armoury 62
   Staffordshire Yeomanry **62**
Owen, Henry 33

Oxbridge Honours Board **15**
Oxbridge Old Wulfrunians **40** – *see also* Old
    Wulfrunians
Oxbridge scholarships 62, 69, 74
Oxford University
    early days 24
    football blues 100
    gender discrimination 130
    headmaster and ushers, requirements of 30
    scholarships 62, 69, 74

Paris 70
Parkfields Comprehensive School 88
part-time staff 27
pay restraint agreements 95
pay scales 51 – *see also* staff salaries
Pebble, The (Glynn Williams) **80–1**
Peer Support 127
Penn Road 33
Philatelic Society 56, 61
Phillips, Gareth
    on co-education 100
    heads of department 78
    Hutton 97
    social mix of school 98
    Taylor's regime 83
photographic society 47
physics 43
Picos **120**
Playboy of the Western World, The (JM Synge)
    71
playground **27**
playing fields 57
Plymley, John 21, 23–4, 136
political economy 44
Powers, Mr **78**
Prague 121
prefects 44, 50, 54, 111
preparatory school 70 – *see also* junior school
prospectus 38, **38**
Protestantism 20, 22
Proverbs, Andy **107**
punishment 54 – *see also* canings; corporal
    punishment; discipline
pupil numbers
    1609 23
    early 19th Century 26, 28
    1844 29
    1854 30
    1863 32
    1865 33

    1867 33
    1868 33
    end of 19th Century 43
    Caldecott's tenure 45
    1920s, second half 57
    1933 60
    1944 64
    1953 70
    1960s 77
    2009–10 126
pure mathematics 44

Quarry Ridge School, Liverpool 74
Queen Square **28**
Queen's Scouts **79** – *see also* Boy Scouts
quincentenary 15, 129

Raby, Mr 21, 136
RAF 14, 54
recusants 22
Red Book 65
redundancies 114
Reformation 20
religious instruction 20, 29
Remove A 50, 57, 65
Remove B 51
Renaissance 20
reports **61**
representative groups 131
Richards' Beau Ideal Cycle Co. Ltd **41**
'Riddles' **46**
Riley, Kevin 100
Riley, RW 65
Roberts, Field Marshal Lord 48
Robertson, William 26, **26**, 136
Robinson, Alfred 46–7, **47**, 50
Rogers, Alan 63
Roman Catholics 22, 26
Roper, John 90, 93
Rover (motor company) 106
Rowlett, Daniel 22, 23, 136
Rowney, AT 50, 59
Royal Air Force 14, 54
Royal Grammar School, Lancaster 32
Royal Grammar School, Newcastle 121
Royal Standard 36
Rugby (school) 30, 40, 127
rugby (sport) **126**
Rushock 18, 20
Rushock Court 18
Rushock estate

declining revenues 42, 43, 51
    Merchant Taylors' accused 22
    mortgaged 36
Rust, Frank 65, **69**, 70, 98
Ryton family 26

salaries, staff – *see* staff salaries
Savage, Thomas 26
school caps 30, **54, 55**, 112
School Certificate 58, 62, 65, 70
school councils 86
School House 33, 44, **56**
school leavers **89, 140–1** – *see also* university
    admissions
school magazine – *see Wulfrunian, The*
school numbers – *see* pupil numbers
school reports **61**
school song 47
science
    1st science master 32, 41
    building programmes needed 45, 71
    humanities and 77
    introduced 42, 43
    laboratory **86**
    learning to learn 118
    mathematics and 51
    Merridale Building **59**
    Taylor 74, 76
    2010 **143**
scientific and mathematical society 47
Scientific Society 61, 62, **67**
scripture 44 – *see also* religious instruction
secondary modern schools 67, 80
Sedgley Park 26
Shakespeare, William 61, 128
'Sharing the Vision' 106, 115
shorthand (subject) 44
sinking fund 68
Sir Thomas Rich's School, Gloucester 83
sixth form
    applicants from other schools 116
    classics **68**
    Common Room **104**
    curriculum choices 78
    enlargement 70
    grammar schools and 77
    library **85**
    photographed **78**
sixth form centre 113, **113**
Stocks's popularity 93
    Taylor 74, 76

Smith, Lawley 60
Smith, William 21
Smyth, RM 40
South Africa 119
South House 44
South Staffordshire coalfield 21
Southwell, John 136
Spitfires 64
sport – *see also* individual sports
  Beach 40
  Caldecott 45
  changing rooms 45, 76
  Hichens 44
  new hall 104, 112–13, **112**
  pavilion 15
  reputation for 14, 40
  Rugby's influence 127
  successful habits 78
Sports Day **42, 56, 122–3, 126**
St Andrew Undershaft 65
St Bartholomew's Medical School 26
St John's College, Cambridge 93
St John's College, Oxford 20
St John's Street
  carved masonry **33**
  dingy surroundings 32
  front of school **31**
  Jenyns provides 18
  plaque **21**
  sale 36
  school opens at 12
  space restrictions 23, 33
St Marylebone Grammar School 93
St Peter's Church
  balcony 12
  Founder's Day **34–5**
  gallery 23, **23**
  gargoyle **23**
  stained glass window **14**
staff photo **99**
staff salaries
  Great Depression 42
  independence 93
  London scale 51
  pay cuts 59
  as proportion of total expenditure 114
Staffordshire County Council 44, 46, 61
Staffordshire Yeomanry **62**
stained glass
  Big School **18, 20, 60, 65, 90**
  St Peter's Church **14**

Standard Assessment Tests (SATS) 118, 127
Stephen Jenyns Library – *see* libraries
Stevenson, Robert Louis 128
Stocks, Tony
  fight against closure 12, 87–8
  fundraising 90
  Hutton and 100
  leaves 93
  listed 136
  photograph **83**
  Rust's concerts 70
  student councils 110
  a teacher first 68, 90
  a tumultuous time 83–4, 86–8, 124
Storre, Francis 22
streaming 86
student bursary fund 15
student councils 110–11
Student Parliament 127
Sunbeam motor cars 44, **44**
superannuation scheme 93
Swallow, JD 61
Switzerland 61

Taming of the Shrew, The (William
  Shakespeare) **61**
Tandy TRS 80s **97**
Tanzania **120**
Taylor, AJP 59
Taylor, Ernest
  appointed 74
  builds on reputation 12
  closing years 80
  depicted **74**
  grammar schools 77
  headmaster's house 76
  heads of department 78
  junior school 76
  listed 136
  Oxbridge 86
  retirement 83
  Wolverhampton Council 82
Taylor, Isaac 24
technical schools 67
tennis 40, **126**
'Tertiolulus' 32
textbooks 23, 77
Thatcher, Margaret 130
think tank 109, 110, 116
Thom & Cuthbertson **41**
Thorpe, John 93

Thurlow, Lord 26
Till, Jeff 70
Timmins, Nicholas
  11-plus 80
  abolition of direct grant schools 98
  Great Depression 41
  Industrial Revolution's effect 27
  Rugby school 30
Tindall, William 28, 136
Tottenham Hotspur FC 45
Tower, The 62, **70**
Trafford, Bernard 108–10
  appointed as head of music 100
  appointed headmaster 106
  Arts Centre 116, **121**
  assisted places scheme 114
  Big Six 117–18
  building programme 111–14
  co-education 112
  extracurricular emphasis 119, 121
  listed 136
  portrait **106**
  pupil numbers 124
  pupils and **108**
  redundancies 114
  reforms under 12
  representative groups 131
  role adopted by 108–10
  student council 110–11
  successor 124
Travellers Club 56, 61, **67**
Treasure Island (Robert Louis Stevenson) 128
Trinity College, Dublin 44
tug of war **56**
Turner JMW **28**
Tyler, Ian 117, 129, **130**

university entrance – *see also* Cambridge
  University; Oxbridge scholarships; Oxford
University
  doubling in fourteen years 70
  open scholarships 56
  proportion going 77, 116, 127
Upton, Chris 25–6, 32, 95, 106
ushers 18, 21, 27, 30, 32

Versailles **67**
Viner, Charles **121**, 128
Viner Arts Centre 128, **129**

Walford, Simon 6, 115

Wall Street Crash 58
Walsall 20
War Memorial Screen **49, 65**
Ward, Judge Malcolm
    assisted places scheme 98, 114
    becomes a governor 87
    on Councillor Bird 88
    government stocks held 90
    on Hutton 99, 104
    job specification for headmaster 95
    photographs **96, 102**
    retires 115
    on Stocks 93
    Trafford 106, 108
weather vane **13**
Wednesfield 20
Wellington College, Berkshire 54
West House 44
Westminster School 112
Westwood, Ernest 93
White, William 28–9, 136
Whitehouse, John **102**, 106, 112
'Who Cares' **129**
Wilde, Oscar 56
Williams, Glynn 80
Williams, Henry 32, 41–2, 106, 136
Williams, Richard 110
Willock, Robert **46**
Wilson, William 136
Winchester School 93
Windsor Great Park 48
Wolverhampton 20–1
    19th Century schools 27, 29
    acceptance of school 36
    business backing for school 90
    Central Town Development Scheme **21**
    Civil War 22
    coal 25, 41
    Distress Committee 45
    early remoteness of 20
    immigration 130
    iron 21, 41, 43
    living costs in 51
    loss of manufacturing industries 26, 124
    Mander on 24
    Merchant Taylors' and 24–5
    overseas markets 26
    population 20, 27, 58, 74

priority to boys from 30
recusants 22
School Board 42
Town Hall 36
Turner, a painting by **28**
unemployment 95, 106
Wolverhampton Chronicle 31
Wolverhampton Council
    alliance with school 42–3
    Combined Cadet Force 79
    Education Committee 82, 87
    grants 46, 61–2
    independence from 82, 97
    initial interest 31
    as local employer 106
    post-severance 92
    severance 88
    strong mutual interest 44
Wolverhampton *Express and Star – see Express and Star*
Wolverhampton Girls' High School 82
Wolverhampton Wanderers FC (Wolves) **82**, 113
women teachers 65
Wood, Roy **107**
Wood, Walter 136
Wood, William 32
Woolley, Randolph 18, **18**
Worcestershire 51
World War I 45, 46, 47–50, 62
World War II 62–6
Wright, David 14
writing (subject) 29
Writing Masters 30
Writing Room 32
Wrottesley, Lord 36
Wulfrunian, The
    1st issue 33, 38
    130 years issue **110**
    1885 **33**
    1905 successes 44
    acknowledged 9
    Black Country 40
    Booth 54
    Caldecott 45
    careers chosen 58
    Combined Cadet Force 70
    Debating Society 40, 61

Derry 57, 70
Hichens 44
Hutton on comprehensive education 96
independence 98
influenza epidemic 50
libraries 84, 86
Merridale Building 59
OTC 48, 62
school societies 61, 78
staff turnover 64
Stocks 93
tone of over the years 38, 40
Trafford's building programme 111–12, 113
War Memorial Screen 49
Williams, Richard 110–11
World War I 48
World War II 62, 63, 64, 66

'Xmasjogathon' 121

Overleaf: WGS Coat of Arms, Big School.